CAST IT OUT

PASTOR GREG LOCKE

Global Vision Press ™

CHARISMA
HOUSE

Cast It Out by Greg Locke
Published by Charisma House, an imprint of Charisma Media
600 Rinehart Road, Lake Mary, Florida 32746
In association with Global Vision Press and Locke Media
2060 Old Lebanon Dirt Road, Mount Juliet, Tennessee 37122

Visit the author's website at lockemedia.org.

Cataloging-in-Publication Data is on file with the Library of Congress.
International Standard Book Number: 978-1-63641-341-9
E-book ISBN: 978-1-63641-342-6

23 24 25 26 27 — 9 8 7 6 5 4 3 2
Printed in the United States of America
Photos and design by Locke Media and Wayne Caparas.

DEDICATION

To my miraculous grandson, Tobias.

*Words cannot express how much love, joy, and excitement you
have brought into our home. It's fitting that my first book about
deliverance be dedicated to you because it was at our very first
National Deliverance Training Conference that your mom and dad
received the call that would change all our lives forever.*

*I wept the first moment I laid hands on you and prayed. I wiped my
eyes and said, "A prophet is born amongst us." I love you so much.
Your grandmother and I cherish every second we get to spend with
you. You are a gift from God, and He will raise you up to change a
generation. You were born into the midst of a revival of signs and
wonders, and it is the delight of my heart to realize that you will
never know anything other than a life of miracles and freedom.*

"Fire of the Holy Ghost, little Chunky. Fire of the Holy Ghost."

The Spirit of the Lord God is upon me; because the Lord hath anointed me to preach good tidings unto the meek; he hath sent me to bind up the brokenhearted, to proclaim liberty to the captives, and the opening of the prison to them that are bound.

—Isaiah 61:1

CONTENTS

FOREWORD

BY ERIC METAXAS

WORDS CANNOT DO justice to how excited I am that my friend Pastor Greg Locke has boldly embraced the biblical and utterly vital ministry of deliverance. But I am perhaps even more excited that he has written this book telling us all about it, because in reading this book more and more of us can see what God Himself is doing in our own time, which is nothing less than breathtaking and deeply encouraging and a cause for rejoicing. This burgeoning move of God in delivering people from demonic oppression is as important as anything could be, so I praise the Lord for all of it and for calling Greg's ministry and this book into existence, because many will find hope and renewed faith as a result.

It is absolutely vital for God's people to understand that one of the main things that often leads people to real faith is their experience with evil, or with the demonic. If you care about evangelism you have to care about deliverance and the subject of demonic evil. That is a part of my own story of coming to faith. That's because when you read about or experience something that is not merely bad but seems genuinely evil, you normally reason that there must be another reality beyond the natural reality most of us have been told is all there is. And you realize that if there is an evil side to that other reality beyond the natural, then there is almost certainly an antidote to it—who happens to be none other than God Himself.

Seeing the evilness of evil drives us to the infinite goodness of God. So suddenly the love of God and the goodness of God become more real than ever because we have seen the horror of what He saves us from. We have seen that He is the only answer to the evil that is real and which we more and more are seeing manifested in the world around us.

We have been living during a time when many "evangelical" churches shrink in fear from these things and even teach that deliverance is a ministry that—although it existed in Jesus' day—no longer is meant to exist in ours. These churches and church leaders seem to want to keep their services "safe" and "respectable" and devoid of any manifestations of the power of God, as though the Aslan of C. S. Lewis' Narnia chronicles really is a "safe" lion rather than the wild—but infinitely good—creature we know him to be. Because of this "domesticated" and unbiblical view of Christian faith, many Christians continue to stumble along in darkness, crippled by emotional wounds, not knowing there is real and tangible hope for them and that by the power of God Himself they might be delivered from the evils that cling to them and hobble them from being who God has called them to be. This blindness on the part of many churches and pastors is of course not God's will, but is Satan's will, and we who claim to know the God of the Bible for who He really is must boldly step up and proclaim the truth and the power of the Holy Spirit to do what God Himself did when He was with us on this planet.

Which is precisely what Greg Locke is doing in this book and elsewhere. There is infinitely more to the Christian life than week after week of taking in vaguely inspiring messages that work hard to avoid the very things that Jesus homed in on throughout His ministry whenever He cast out demons and healed the sick and the blind and raised the dead and turned over tables and denounced corruption and the wickedness of religious leaders who gave lip-service to God but were far from Him in their hearts.

So I rejoice to see the ministry of Greg Locke and the appearance of this book, which herald nothing less than a new move of God in our own time. Just as the Jesus Revolution which focused on evangelism fifty years ago came out of nowhere, and just as in the 1950s there was a sudden upsurge in Christian leaders ministering in the realm of supernatural healing, so today we are seeing something new and wonderful and powerful and deeply needed in the realm of deliverance. Because of it, more and more believers will be set free and able to act like the actual church of Jesus Christ on earth, which is never respectable or tame, but which is always doing the powerful things that Jesus Himself did.

I would be remiss if I didn't mention my dear friend Ken Fish as central to my own reawakening on this subject. In the last decade I had the privilege of getting to know him and watching him minister in healing and deliverance in a way I'd never seen with my own eyes. It was astonishing to witness someone actually doing what I knew was biblical, but which I simply hadn't seen much of at all in any churches. But the more I saw in Ken's ministry the more I cried out for God to raise up others besides Ken who could do what he was doing. The need was so great that unless God raised up others to minister in deliverance as my friend Ken was heroically doing, millions would simply continue along in their bondage, never knowing there was hope and freedom for them.

So you can imagine my joy when I learned that Greg Locke was at the center of those who are right now being raised up, knowing that he has the zeal and fearlessness not just to minister in the power of the Holy Spirit along these lines, but to tell others about it and lead them into participating in it too, by teaching them about it from a biblical viewpoint, as he does in this wonderful book. So yes, the Lord is at work right now. And this is only the beginning, with much more to come just ahead. Look for it, and don't miss the opportunity to be a part of it yourself. Hallelujah. Amen.

Eric Metaxas
New York City, June 2023

INTRODUCTION

Y ou wouldn't be holding this book if the Lord hadn't in some way prompted you to read it, so I'll ask you right off the top to put aside any notion you have about deliverance ministry—or about me, for that matter. The Holy Spirit is moving through our church, across this nation, and all around the world with a sense of urgency that hasn't been seen since the day of Pentecost, and His mission is as clear as day—He wants to set the captives free. In these last of the last days, He has snatched me, my family, and our entire church out of dead, powerless religion to serve as a sign and an example of the supernatural outpouring of His Spirit. We simply said, "Yes, Lord, send us," and two years later here we are, casting out demons and seeing miraculous healings like there's no tomorrow.

Let me tell you what the biblical essence and definition of deliverance ministry really is. It's not all the hokey pokey spooky stuff that you may have heard of in the past or seen on Netflix. It's simply this: submit to God; resist the devil, and he will flee from you (Jas. 4:7). In this book, we're going to address these commands—and that promise—in a way that should truly equip you for each. And, of course, the only way to do that is to explore how Jesus did it and how He taught it. For that, this is a book about the supernatural deliverance ministry of Jesus and what it should look like today.

Part 1 of this book is titled "The Deliverance Awakening," which explains how the Holy Spirit took us from a tiny, politically charged church into a full-blown move of God that is already reaching all nations. Part 2 is titled "Jesus on Deliverance," where we will let Jesus add some meat to the bones of Part 1. And Part 3 is titled "Further Demystifying Deliverance," which will do just that. Through it all, you will see the scarlet thread of the blood of Jesus and the testimony of the saints of God woven through every chapter. I trust it will bless you.

PART 1

THE DELIVERANCE AWAKENING

Chapter 1

HOW DID THIS HAPPEN TO US?

But the natural man receiveth not the things of the Spirit of God: for they are foolishness unto him: neither can he know them, because they are spiritually discerned.

—1 CORINTHIANS 2:14

O N A SUNDAY morning in 2021, I preached a message called "The Season of Getting Serious." I had no idea that three days from that moment, on a Wednesday night, I would give my first deliverance message. I look back now and understand it was absolutely providential. Little did I know when I preached on the *season of getting serious* that our church was about to get really serious about a part of Jesus' ministry that nobody seems to want to be serious about.

My wife, Tai, and I were about to lead our church across a chasm that was all but untouchable in my Baptist theology. We were standing on a precipice leaning into a high-risk leap of faith, knowing every demon on earth and under the earth was waiting for us to fall. But we clearly knew what the Holy Spirit of God was telling us, so we simply obeyed.

Setting people free through deliverance has never been about the charismatic personality of the person with the pen or the microphone. It is always about the power and authority of the name of Jesus and the Word of God through the indwelling of the Holy Spirit. For nearly three decades as a seminary-trained preacher, the

1

fullness of that power escaped me. But from that Wednesday night onward, everything began to change—especially my relationship with the Holy Spirit.

> But the Comforter, which is the Holy Ghost, whom the Father will send in my name, he shall teach you all things, and bring all things to your remembrance, whatsoever I have said unto you.
>
> —JESUS (JOHN 14:26)

THE SEASON OF GETTING SERIOUS

When we decided to keep our church open at the onset of the government-mandated lockdowns due to the COVID breakout, out of necessity and caution we started meeting in the parking lot, and we never could have imagined what God was actually doing. A historically devastating tornado had just ripped through Nashville the week before and obliterated large swatches of our community in Mount Juliet. For this, we were already in emergency response mode, as we were the only large church in the area that escaped major damage, so we joined forces with the first responders and immediately served as an emergency supply center and refuge for those who lost their homes.

At that time, Global Vision Bible Church was still meeting in our three-hundred-seat chapel, which was the same building we used as a sanctuary for the homeless. We had a very small campus at the time, and it was honestly all we had to work with. We knew there was no way we were going to cancel church, nor would we curtail our emergency response efforts, so we decided to hold services in the parking lot and keep the chapel open to the people in need of sanctuary or supplies.

When the COVID mandates were first handed down, we honestly weren't trying to be defiant. We were simply standing in obedience to God for the sake of the hurting and homeless in our community, so we had no choice but to push back. No mandate of man was going to stop us from obeying the Lord. We immediately realized that the Lord had set our church apart to stand firm while most others bowed to the powers that be, and we absolutely would not forsake "the assembling of ourselves together" (Heb. 10:25)—come what may.

When the word got out on social media, people started coming from everywhere, and the news media went ballistic. Some were flying drones around saying, "Oh my goodness, they're going to kill everyone in town!" It's important to note that we never brought any death to this town, not even one soul, praise God. Instead, we brought new life where bones were formerly dead and dry. In those first days of the crisis, I was preaching on a picnic table and then on a truck bed out under the elements.

When Resurrection Sunday brought a heavy downpour and folks chose to stand out in the rain (which was a beautiful sight to see), I realized we needed to provide the people with some cover, so we got a big tent that sat a whopping 650. We honestly thought there was no way we would ever fill it, but on the first Sunday—*boom!*—standing room only. We tried to ride it out with that size tent for about a month, but there were just too many people showing up.

At that point, Tai and I discussed all our options, and we realized the Lord wanted us to continue meeting in one large group rather than breaking into multiple services as we had while meeting in the chapel, so we took what felt like a huge risk at the time and brought in an even larger tent. While Tai was already there, I thought we were being overly bold in our faith, and I've got to admit that I battled a lot of doubt at the time. But we knew the Lord was at work through every bit of this, so we pressed on.

We were about two weeks into the larger tent, and *boom!*—it happened again. Every time we bought a bigger tent, within a couple of services Tai would say, "The tent isn't big enough, babe." And I'd be thinking, "Are you kidding me? Why didn't you tell me that before we bought this one? You're prophesying a little late, baby!" And we pressed on, eventually moving up to the 1,250-seat red-and-white-striped "circus tent" made iconic by the global news media. It was honestly the only tent of that size that we could quickly acquire at a price we could afford. While the media feasted on it as a derision, to us it was a prophetic symbol of the healing place we would soon become.

In those days, the tent was set up along the highway with cars zooming by directly behind the preaching platform. It was super distracting and even a bit dangerous, but the Lord just kept bringing in the people and covering us through every challenge. Folks started driving in from every state in America, and many were flying in from all corners of the world. It was crazy, but we just kept riding it out and praying through every step of it.

MY FIRST OPEN VISION

And it shall come to pass in the last days, saith God, I will pour out of my Spirit upon all flesh: and your sons and your daughters shall prophesy, and your young men shall see visions, and your old men shall dream dreams.

—ACTS 2:17

By the time we extended the red-and-white tent to seat 1,550, I thought we would never need another tent. That thing felt bigger than Noah's ark, and I honestly believed the crowds would soon start growing weary of all the scrutiny while meeting outside. The summer temperatures were in the high nineties, we could hear the roosters crowing next door, the police were showing up every week to deal with protestors, media cameras were everywhere, and the traffic and parking situation had become a nightmare. It was often overwhelming. I just couldn't see how we could possibly sustain all of it, so I took my prayer life to another level, and things began to break in me.

One day I was in my office being still before the Lord, and He started working on me in ways I never could have imagined. You've got to understand that I wasn't flowing in any of the spiritual gifts at this point. I was still Baptist with a capital *B*. I was Baptist born, Baptist bred, and when I died, I'd be Baptist dead—or so I thought. Before this moment, even while the church was growing in biblical fashion, every time things would look like they were getting ready to break loose in the Spirit, I'd sheepishly hold it back. Without realizing what I was actually doing, I'd quench it. I'd be like, "No, uh-uh. I'm not allowing wildfire to break out in my service." But let me tell you something about wildfire: there are always enough wet blankets around to quickly put it out. Back then, I was chief among them.

In my office on that momentous day, as I looked out the window, God shocked me with the first open vision of my life. I have been preaching since I was sixteen years old—sixteen thousand sermons all over the world in forty-eight states and fifteen foreign countries—yet I'd never flowed in any of the gifts with recognition of them and certainly never had a prophetic vision that I was aware of. I had just completed the first edition of the first book in this trilogy, *Weapons of Our Warfare*. This vision and the events that followed gave birth to the second book, *Accessing Your Anointing*.

I need you to know that my previous ignorance of the gifts wasn't an indication that I was wicked or faithless. I had simply never learned how it all worked or where it all really came from, and I definitely didn't want to overturn my lifelong, ironclad theology, so I always swept over the subject in dismissive/religious fashion—just as I was taught. I had been raised as a strict cessationist, and I was seminary trained to believe all the gifts died with the apostles, so all my study of Scripture and all my sermons were fashioned to agree with that false doctrine. Coming out of seminary, I was an aggressive champion of cessationist thought. I even wrote a book from that worldview, so the book on this subject had long been closed. I address it all with great detail in *Accessing Your Anointing*, so I won't belabor the point here. Suffice it to say the Holy Ghost changed all that.

When I looked out the window that day and scanned up the

hillside, at first I saw nothing but woods. Then, suddenly a clearing appeared, and on it was a massive white tent, twice the size of the former red-and-white one. It was a stunning sight, and it was as real to my eyes as the big circus tent. At the time I wasn't at all interested in expanding the tent again. I loved that tent, but I couldn't unsee what the Lord was showing me. So I called the tent guys and said, "God told me to buy a big white tent that seats three thousand people and to put it in the woods."

They answered, "When do you want it there?"

I said, "I'd like it there this Sunday, but I know that's not possible, so let's get some bulldozers in here, and I'll start raising some money."

To God be the glory, it all happened. We went from a 300-seat chapel to a 650-seat tent to a 3,000-seat tent in just over a year, and (at the time of writing this book) we have baptized more than 8,500 converts in a horse trough—because the gospel still works, and the Lord still speaks.

It's not like I was looking for another move of God; on the contrary. We were in the middle of a revival that most churches and their pastors would die for. People were traveling in by the thousands, and unprecedented levels of generosity were flowing to us and through us. The Lord had marked us as good stewards and blessed us magnanimously. Through our bold giving and risk-taking in the face of all the storms, I learned that the Father is not just looking for a church He can bless; He's looking for a church He can trust. And when He finds a people He can trust, He *will* bless them. We are greatly blessed. Please take this sidebar to heart—if you're a good steward with a little, you'll be an even better steward with a lot, and the more you give, the more it will be given back to you (Luke 6:38). So be boldly generous with what you have, and watch what the Lord will do.

That's all we really did, and in return the Lord sent revival in the midst of revival—and blew our minds. I honestly wasn't looking for it. I wasn't even praying about it. And to be totally transparent with you, had I known then how it would eventually turn my theology upside down, I may even have been praying against it.

At the time I had all the arguments against signs and wonders firmly in hand, and deliverance ministry wasn't even an afterthought, as I had predetermined it all to be nothing more than foolish, hyped-up "charismaniac" nonsense. But then God said, "I'm going to remove your denominational lenses, and I'm going to show you what the Bible really says." He poured out His Spirit on me and on our church (Acts 2:17).

Suddenly, people started getting healed in our tent and online across the live stream, and I simply didn't know what to do with it. Miracles and wonders abounded, so we just let the Holy Spirit show up and show out and watched as God got His glory in amazing ways. We listened for His voice, and we committed to following Him no matter where He led us.

> My sheep hear my voice, and I know them, and they follow me.
> —Jesus (John 10:27)

Just a few weeks into the new tent, a rare December tornado hit Mount Juliet. Unlike the one that got all this started, this one seemed to target us as it ripped through our tent and left it on the ground in shambles. While our detractors celebrated our moment of hardship, we were undaunted. We dragged fifteen hundred chairs out from under the wreckage, set them up neatly in a fresh part of the parking lot (that had just that week been cleared), and got ready for church. We were back out under the elements, this time in the dead of winter, and people still joyfully showed up by the hundreds in their puffer coats. Some even got baptized despite 22-degree temperatures. It was freezing cold outside, and they just kept coming. Our people were being tested, and once again they rose to the occasion. After clearing more land to establish a more level foundation, we moved back into the repaired and repositioned tent with great anticipation for what the Lord would do next.

What Are We Going to Do With This?

When we published *Accessing Your Anointing*, folks started sending me links to videos dealing with the gifts and the demonstration of miracles. Then one of our security guys asked if I had ever heard of a guy named Isaiah Saldivar, and I had not. I pulled up a clip of him on YouTube, and I was genuinely moved. He might have been the skinniest thing I've ever laid eyes on, and he was much younger than I had anticipated, but he was also one of the most passionate preachers I've ever heard in my life.

The more videos I watched of Isaiah and his contemporaries, the more people I saw crying out and manifesting evil spirits. I thought this was only going on in back rooms and other shadowy places, but it was happening in broad daylight—in churches and out of churches—among people from all walks of life. It was eye-opening. Though I was no longer a scoffer, I still couldn't imagine myself doing what these men and women of God were doing. I knew Jesus did it, and I knew the apostle Paul and even Philip the evangelist did it. But me? Nope.

Tai and I kept on watching, and we also started researching these folks and all the biblically sound writings we could find on the subject. Have you ever heard the saying that if you hang around the barbershop long enough, you get a haircut? It's true. These men and women of God were saying and writing things I couldn't deny. Every time my cessationist mind tried to say, "That's not in the Bible," the Lord showed me that it was clearly in the Bible. For that, we had to ask ourselves: What are we going to do with this?

Before we take our deep dive into the tragically dismissed subject of this book, I want to continue sharing how God used people and circumstances to open us to the revelation of biblical deliverance, so I'm going to rewind a couple months and explain. If you've seen *Come Out in Jesus Name* you'll be familiar with the timeline, but I need to fill in some important twists and turns that might help you see how God softened my heart and remolded me for this mission.

If you're still struggling with doubt, maybe you'll soon see yourself going through a similar process on the Potter's wheel.

> But now, O LORD, you are our Father; we are the clay, and you are our potter; we are all the work of your hand.
>
> —ISAIAH 64:8, ESV

A DEMON MANIFESTS DURING THE LIVE STREAM

Our journey into deliverance actually started during a service just before the tornado tore down our tent. We were baptizing folks as we always do, and things were moving along beautifully—until the unthinkable happened. Our live stream has a large following, and I'm always sensitive to the folks on both sides of the camera, but on this occasion I simply didn't know what to do. As embarrassing as it was, had it not happened, we wouldn't be where we are as a church today.

A grandmother jumped into the baptismal pool, and to my surprise she had an eight- or nine-year-old girl in her arms. I'd never performed a double-dippin' baptism before, but I could see in Grandma's eyes that she was dead earnest in her intent. She wanted me to dip them both at the same time, and I wasn't going to embarrass that precious lady in front of the church or the folks on the live stream. I could sense there was something deeper going on, and I knew at the very least that Grandma was carrying a burden for that little girl.

As I put her down into the water, Grandma went under nice and smooth, but the little girl put her hands on both sides of that baptistery, lifted herself up, and manifested a full-blown cat right in church, screeching and all. In that moment, I realized the little girl was manifesting a demon. She was hissing and even put her fingers out like claws. In all my years of ministry all around the world, I'd never seen anything like it. I looked at Tai, and her eyes were bigger than two Jimmy Dean sausage patties. I was thinking, "What in the world do I do with this?"

At that moment, I was afraid of the little girl and what she might do next. She looked ten feet tall and bulletproof. Keep in mind, this was back before I began studying biblical deliverance, and I hadn't yet watched any videos on the subject, so I had never knowingly seen a demon manifest before. I had heard about it and even preached that we have the power to cast out demons, but I didn't really believe it in a literal sense.

We eventually helped Grandma and the little girl climb out of the tub, and I just tried to return to dipping folks as if nothing happened. I kept thinking, "That didn't happen; that didn't happen." Oh, but it happened! Tai was holding the microphone for me as I did the dipping, but she quickly handed it to someone else on the team and said, "I'm gonna go find that little girl." She then searched through the crowd and even looked out in the parking lot, but they were nowhere to be found.

That night things got serious in my house. As we lay in bed, Tai started weeping and said, "How could we not know how to help that little girl? We pastor a church—a big church, a successful church—we've got best-selling books, podcasts, and three million followers on the internet, but we can't even face a demon in an eight-year-old child?" We cried long and hard. Then we held hands and prayed about it, and we continued praying about it every night for two weeks, always weeping before the Lord. We were praying about things that would risk all that the Lord had built during this amazing season of growth and revival, so it was a daunting time. Through it all we learned that deliverance ministry will get really practical really quick and will suddenly show you what you've been missing in the Spirit—once you truly open your eyes.

As we considered what was coming, I'll admit I was apprehensive. Tai, on the other hand, was not. I adore my wife, and the Holy Spirit knew that her early conviction would in turn convict me. He knew my heart would follow Him wherever He was taking her. He knew He had to cut me to my heart to move me because I had too much religion in me to just lay it all down over a single issue.

My love for my wife in effect stripped away my religious pride and helped me tear down those strongholds.

As mentioned in the film, Tai purchased the book *The Secrets to Deliverance* by Alexander Pagani, and the way Pagani laid it out was so biblically sound and simple that it pretty well sealed the deal. The Lord was clearly preparing us for a total reformation of our ministry. From there, we began to pray, "Lord, if You'll bring people in our path who are demonized, and if You'll show us who they are, we'll do it. It might take us a while to get it going, but we'll do it." We didn't initially tell anybody we were praying about it—not our congregation, and not even our staff. Little did we know the Lord had been preparing the church long before He prepared me.

> My son, if thou wilt receive my words, and hide my commandments with thee; so that thou incline thine ear unto wisdom, and apply thine heart to understanding; yea, if thou criest after knowledge, and liftest up thy voice for understanding; if thou seekest her as silver, and searchest for her as for hid treasures; then shalt thou understand the fear of the LORD, and find the knowledge of God.
>
> —PROVERBS 2:1–5

Chapter 2

STRANGE MANIFESTATIONS

And they went out and preached every-
where, while the Lord worked with them and con-
firmed the message by accompanying signs.
—MARK 16:20, ESV

S TILL CATCHING OUR breath from all this spiritual upheaval, we embarked on the book tour for *Accessing Your Anointing*, which was basically my very public goodbye to cessationism. As we traveled around for the two weeks leading up to Christmas, through every night of the tour, weird things happened that had never happened to me before. Most profoundly, on the road from our first stop in Dallas to our second stop in Louisiana, Tai called me in the middle of the night with the shocking news that the tent had been torn down by a tornado.

I almost canceled the tour, but Tai insisted she could rally the troops to get us ready for Sunday in the parking lot, and the Holy Spirit convinced me that this was a moment He had ordained for her to shine as a general—and boy, did she. We both could discern that the enemy was trying to stop what the Lord had planned for the tour, so instead of giving in to the attack, we set our faces like flint and grew even more expectant. I got back to Global Vision just in time for our first winter service in the parking lot, and once we finished the baptisms, Tai and a couple more members of our team climbed on board the bus for the remainder of the tour.

That night we drove up to Owensboro, Kentucky, for our first church stop on the tour. While I was preaching, people started screaming and raising their hands in an unusual way. Once they calmed down, a few folks started moaning in the back of the auditorium, and I didn't know what to make of it. Our host, Pastor Brian Gibson, later came to me and said, "Something is different about you. Have you been praying about something serious?"

I acknowledged his impression without spilling the beans, and he said, "I don't know what it is, but I'm gonna tell you right now, when you walked in the room tonight, things just started manifesting themselves. There's something different about you, and I believe God's about to take you to a new stratosphere."

At the time I sincerely couldn't imagine what that might mean. Everything I had seen about deliverance ministry was well below the radar, so I didn't give it a lot of thought. The next night we went to another church, and lo and behold, the pastor was talking about deliverance. I thought it was too odd to be a simple coincidence (if there is such a thing), but I chose not to say anything. The next night we were at Pastor Shannon Williams' church, Finish Line Christian Center in North Carolina, and at the last minute I felt led to preach on Mark 9:29: "This kind can come out by nothing but prayer and fasting" (NKJV).

I hadn't begun teaching on deliverance ministry, but I could sense there was something that needed to "come out" of some of the people in the auditorium, just as was the case in the previous two churches. I was still hesitant to admit this to anyone, but it was becoming impossible to keep it down while I was preaching in the Spirit.

The next night we were at Pastor Henry Shaffer's church in Aiken, South Carolina. Once I finished my sermon on Jonah, the pastor asked me to join him in his office to talk. There was a sense of tension in the air, and it felt like I was about to be scolded in the principal's office. Henry immediately said, "I want to talk to you about something, and I don't even know what I'm going to tell you, but I want to talk to you about deliverance ministry."

Inside I was like, "You've got to be kidding me."

Henry went on to tell me the Holy Spirit had told him to take the front row out of his church and to fill it with folks in wheelchairs and said, "If you'll believe in deliverance and start to cast out the spirit of infirmity, people will get up and walk and be healed in the name of Jesus."

As I sat there, I thought, "This cannot be accidental; it has to be providential." Meanwhile, my wife had found this book about deliverance in Henry's bookstore while she and the team waited for my meeting to wrap up. When we got on the bus, we could hardly wait to swap notes. This was happening every night.

Shortly after we wrapped the tour, a package came in the mail from Pastor Shannon Williams' wife, Nancy, who happened to work for Derek Prince Ministries. The package contained Prince's book *They Shall Expel Demons*, which I'd bought five years earlier without regard to the author but never cracked open for fear a devil would jump out. Nancy also sent a five-CD set of Prince's teachings on deliverance. At this point I was still like, "Derek who?" I didn't even know what his voice sounded like. I actually anticipated that he might have been a redneck like me.

When I turned on the CD and heard this Greek scholar teaching with his beautiful British accent, I couldn't wait to dive in. Tai and I would just drive around the Tennessee countryside and listen to those CDs day after day. We were amazed by what this man was saying. We kept saying over and over throughout the series, "This is what we're experiencing! This is what we're seeing in the churches!" So every day we listened, and listened again, as we continued to pray and fast.

God Prepared the Sheep
Before the Shepherd

> Shepherd the flock of God that is among you, exercising over-
> sight, not under compulsion, but willingly, as God would have
> you; not for shameful gain, but eagerly; not domineering over
> those in your charge, but being examples to the flock.
> —1 Peter 5:2–3, esv

Though we had already started flowing in some of the gifts of the Spirit, as did the Global Vision congregation, deliverance had yet to break out. Most folks in our church started out as cessationist as I was, so the notion of getting thousands of folks at different stages of their walk to see what we were seeing was beyond daunting. I know they trusted my biblical understanding, but this was new territory, and I knew such a dramatic shift in our theology would risk losing many if not most. It would also bring overwhelming levels of hatred and rejection from the cessationist crowd. But I'm called to feed the sheep, not to slop the hogs or entertain the goats, so I knew it had to be done.

Shortly after finishing Prince's book, I told Tai I was ready to start a sermon series on deliverance from demons and just let the chips fall where they may. She was *all in*. I'll never forget that first service. When I finally said, "I believe the Lord wants me to preach on deliverance from demons," to my great surprise, our church went nuts. I mean, they roared with approval. You would have thought I'd told them that everyone was getting a free car!

At that moment I realized that God in His mercy had prepared the hearts of the sheep before He ever prepared the heart of the shepherd. He instantly relieved me of all my fears, as many of them were way ahead of me in this regard. For the pastors and ministry folks reading this book, let me encourage you. Don't ever underestimate the hunger of the people for the supernatural gifts of the Holy Spirit. The sooner you realize they're waiting for you, the better.

I preached that first message on deliverance with fire and conviction and walked out of the tent that night knowing it wouldn't be long before the Lord would challenge me to actually cast out a demon. I remember thinking, "How on earth can I be so convicted about something I've never done?" The prospect was even more unnerving than that first sermon, but I knew it was coming.

THEN IT HAPPENED

> Jesus said unto him, If thou canst believe, all things are possible to him that believeth. And straightway the father of the child cried out, and said with tears, Lord, I believe; help thou mine unbelief.
>
> —MARK 9:23–24

After that first deliverance sermon, I immediately got on the bus, and we drove six or seven hours over to Arkansas, where I preached at a tent that seated about six hundred people. The place was packed despite it being so freezing cold that I was surprised anybody stayed. The service went on and on, and it was beautiful. Just before I got up to speak, a lady came to my book table and said, "Pastor Locke, you're my online pastor. I love you; thank you for your stand. I appreciate your boldness. I drove all the way here tonight from Oklahoma because I need deliverance."

I nervously said, "Oh no, ma'am, you should have found a deliverance minister in Oklahoma before you came to Arkansas. I've never done that." Can you imagine? I just didn't think I was ready.

But she said, "I know; I watch every sermon, and I pay close attention to every word that comes out of your mouth. I told you, you're my online pastor, and I'm telling you right now I'm your guinea pig. The Holy Ghost told me to come here tonight to get some deliverance from you. I need it that bad. I'm so desperate that I'll stay till three in the morning in the cold if I have to, but you're gonna have to pray over me before I leave!" Again, can you imagine? I was nervous as a long-tailed cat in a room full of rocking chairs, so I just said OK and headed for the platform to preach.

My message that night was about the lukewarm church from Revelation chapter 3. All the while as I preached I was thinking to myself, "I hope she gets offended or has some sort of emergency and just has to leave." I was that nervous. When I got through preaching, I went back to the book table where it's customary to shake hands with folks and sign some books and get some pictures taken. I dragged it out as long as I could. I guarantee you I spent an hour and a half standing in the meet-and-greet line, and she patiently sat there in her little seat in that freezing cold tent with her husband and sister by her side.

When I finally ran out of people and realized my delay tactic had failed, I took a deep breath and walked over to the woman. My heart felt like it was about to beat out of my chest, and I simply said, "Well, here we go, ma'am." I pray for thousands of people every week, but it's never felt like this. I've discovered that it requires an entirely different level of faith to *truly* walk in the authority that God has given you, and before that night I hadn't realized I had that kind of authority.

I then said, "Are you ready?"

And she said, "Are *you* ready?"

And I was thinking, *That's to be determined.* Then I said, "Just bow your head"—not because that was necessary, but because I didn't really know what else to say or do! For that moment I felt as dumb as a box of bricks. I had read all those books and listened to all of Derek Prince's CDs, but I'd never really spent time thinking about the "how to" part of it all. I didn't know any spirit names. I had yet to truly study Leviathan or Jezebel or their ilk. And I certainly didn't have a deliverance manual to reference. But I knew how Jesus and the disciples did it, so I just tried to keep it simple. I put my hand on her and said, "Evil spirit, I don't know who you are, but you come out right now in the name of Jesus." The woman immediately slumped out of her chair, hit the floor, and started convulsing. I thought, "You gotta be kidding me! It can happen that quick?"

Then I said, "In the name of Jesus, come out right now. You hear me? You hear me, you foul devil? You hear me, you foul spirit? You better come up and out right now. You're coming all the way up and all the way out. I don't know what your name is, but I'll stay here all night. You come out right now in the name of Jesus!" At this point the woman was wallowing around on the ground screaming and throwing up all kinds of white foamy stuff. Then she suddenly stood up, squalling and crying out, "I'm free! I'm free!" She immediately started praising God and using her prayer language while hugging her sister and husband. Then she looked at me and said, "My back is straight. I've been freed from the heaviness. I've been freed from infirmity. I've been freed tonight!"

On the ride back home, I felt like a little kid. I kept saying to the guys on the bus, "It works! It's not just a theory, it actually works!"

> And Jesus rebuked the demon, and it came out of him, and the boy was healed instantly.
>
> —MATTHEW 17:18, ESV

SET FREE IN JESUS' NAME

That Sunday at Global Vision I preached part two of deliverance from demons. In my message I explained that the process of casting out demons hasn't changed since Jesus first taught us how to do it. It certainly helped that I had just lived that reality. At the end of the service, well after my sermon, I felt compelled to share what happened in Arkansas. I went through the whole shebang, and the church exploded with joyful excitement. One verifiable testimony was all it took.

Immediately after the service a man approached me and said he had driven down from Michigan to see if we could help deliver him from his addiction to pornography. I pulled him down close to the floor with me and said, "Spirit of lust, come out in Jesus' name," and the man immediately convulsed to the ground, and it was on. Deliverance ministry simply began breaking out at Global Vision.

We were total rookies, and we just trusted the Holy Spirit to lead us through it. We hadn't even contemplated the existence of a trained deliverance team, so we just started praying over people, and church went until 2:30. At the time, it was the longest Sunday service in the history of our church. I was so tired I couldn't see straight, but the Lord sustained me.

The next Sunday we ministered to folks in need of deliverance until midnight. We worked for fourteen-plus hours straight in a cold tent, and again the Lord sustained us. People were literally waiting in line, and we really didn't know what to do but pray for them as I had the woman in Arkansas and the man from Michigan. We were still just a week into it, so we had only a handful of people that had any training at all.

I had a John Eckhardt manual in one hand and a Bible in the other, and I'd simply ask, "What are you struggling with?" From there we just started calling it out, and demons would manifest right before our eyes. The people waiting in line were watching too, knowing all the while that they were next. These hurting folks were watching someone writhe around on the ground, and still they waited anxiously for their chance to get free. At the time it was the craziest thing I'd ever been a part of, yet it was just the beginning.

When the third Sunday came around, we ministered to folks until 2:30 the next morning. It was beyond amazing. Word was getting out, and hurting people of all types were showing up every day of the week. When the fourth Sunday ran past midnight, I realized we had no choice but to start working smarter, not harder, so we immediately prayed for a divine strategy. The very next day a package came that contained a book called *Battling the Hosts of Hell: The Diary of an Exorcist* by a deceased Baptist preacher named Win Worley. After flipping through it, I learned he had some old videos on YouTube that showed him leading mass deliverance services, and to God be the glory, we had our marching orders.

A MOVE OF GOD

For freedom Christ has set us free; stand firm therefore, and
do not submit again to a yoke of slavery.

—GALATIANS 5:1, ESV

In very short order we had a well-trained team of deliverance ministers showing up every Sunday night at 6 p.m. to help Tai and me
set people free. A year later, what started as an experiment has
turned into seventy straight Sunday nights and counting. Nearly
every member of our church has found freedom and healing in
these services, and many hundreds travel in from all over the world,
every single week.

We've held multiple deliverance conferences where more than
three thousand participate in a single Sunday night deliverance service. We've witnessed countless healings of every sort of disorder
and disease (stage IV cancer included), and we've seen thousands of
lives instantly transformed in ways that simply cannot be explained
outside of the gospel of Jesus Christ.

We then locked shields with generals of deliverance ministry
who had been at it much longer than we had. We shared our bur-
dens and our victories in beautiful ways. Alexander Pagani, Isaiah
Saldivar, Vlad Savchuk, Mike Signorelli, Daniel Adams, Henry
Shaffer, Leon Du Preez, and Jenny Weaver have each come to our
tent to help train our people, prophesy over us, and—of course—
cast out demons in Jesus' name. Every week the Lord sends more
allies to join us in this spiritual war, and word of this movement is
beginning to reach all nations.

On the night we premiered *Come Out in Jesus Name* in theaters
nationwide, we again joined forces with our fellow demon slayers
to hold the largest and most powerful mass deliverance in history,
as nearly 80,000 people rocked the world with their testimonies of
deliverance and healing on social media. A month later another

120,000 souls were also awakened to power and commissioned to set people free, and so it continues.

Now that I've testified to all that the Lord is doing in our midst, I hope to share the biblical truth and inspired revelations the Lord used to erase all my doubts. I am a voracious reader of great Christian writers, but even more, I'm an unashamed Bible scholar. I've invested my entire life into reading and studying and teaching the Bible, and I consider this to be my most important work yet. If you stick with me through the conclusion, I believe you'll find biblical answers to your most pressing deliverance questions and will soon feel equipped to help everyone you know find true freedom and healing in Christ—starting with you.

This is a true move of God, and we believe it is the beginning of the most important awakening in the history of Christianity. When you come to the realization that more than a third of Jesus' ministry (the casting out of demons) has been virtually ignored for two thousand years—along with His commission for all believers to do the same—and suddenly the Holy Spirit activates this ministry in all corners of the world, it would be foolish to minimize the implications. Everyone likes to ask "What would Jesus do?" until it's time to actually do what Jesus did. Well, body of Christ, it's time.

> Truly, truly, I say to you, whoever believes in me will also do the works that I do; and greater works than these will he do, because I am going to the Father.
>
> —JESUS (JOHN 14:12, ESV)

Chapter 3

WE EITHER BELIEVE THE BIBLE OR WE DON'T

But be doers of the word, and not hearers only,
deceiving yourselves.

—JAMES 1:22, ESV

W E ALL NEED to understand that the Bible is still just as practical and prophetic today as it was when the ink of inspiration flowed out in Revelation 22. We also have to realize that we have no say in which parts of the Bible to obey. We either believe the Bible or we don't, and the only parts of the Bible we truly believe are the parts we truly *behave*.

In this chapter I'm going to explain what has become one of the most controversial passages in the Bible, Mark 16:15–18, where Jesus delivers the Great Commission as recorded by Mark. This passage has often divided the church, and much of it has been egregiously ignored by many denominations. It won't take long for me to explain why this has happened, and all I'll need are the words of Jesus to do so. The Bible will always explain itself.

Jesus is just as powerful and anointed a teacher today as He was when He walked the earth, and He is doing the same things today that He has always done. Jesus was the Word then, and He is still the Word now. If we have a problem applying Jesus and His teachings to our lives today, the problem resides in us and our religion. That's the realization the Holy Spirit used to break me of mine.

Having been an evangelist for ten years and then a pastor for another fifteen years, I've often found myself trying to read certain things *into* the Bible and also *out of* the Bible because of the way I was taught. I found myself apologizing for the clear teaching of the Bible, but I was never trying to deceive the people or lead them astray. Thank God, He has brought me into a new understanding.

He That Believeth

And he said unto them, Go ye into all the world, and preach the gospel to every creature. He that believeth and is baptized shall be saved; but he that believeth not shall be damned. And these signs shall follow them that believe; in my name shall they cast out devils; they shall speak with new tongues; they shall take up serpents; and if they drink any deadly thing, it shall not hurt them; they shall lay hands on the sick, and they shall recover.

—Mark 16:15–18

Here in our key passage of this study Jesus is at the end of His ministry, preparing to ascend to the right hand of the Father. No one has a problem with how it starts, but there are certain commands that follow this instruction that most Christians have been ignoring for a very long time because we were told to look past them. Much of this ignorance is rooted in the cessationist theology that we dismantled in *Accessing Your Anointing*, so though I'll address all the major objections to deliverance ministry throughout this book, suffice it here to say that the commands of Jesus and the power of God must never be discounted or diminished, let alone ignored.

It's a tragedy that many large denominations continue teaching that the gifts Jesus addresses in this passage no longer apply to us today, so I want to give it a solid study before moving on. For some of you, it may be your first unadulterated look. I know people who have become so incredibly bitter and discouraged over this passage and others like it that they now deal with deep depression. Some have even taken their own lives, all because they could not reconcile what the Bible clearly says with what their grandfather or their ex-pastor told them it says. In these last of the last days, it's time to take off the denominational lens and learn to read the Bible exactly as it was written.

Many of us have been taught to question the validity and authority of the Bible and to force false assumptions to make sense when they clearly do not make sense. Someone new to the Bible might be shocked to learn that this crescendo of a passage containing the Great Commission of Jesus is so widely ignored. The fact that it contains the most indisputable command to cast out demons found in the entire Bible might make that an understandable distinction for cessationists, but that's just a small part of the controversy. This passage is fully packed with words that trigger religious division. For that, let's take a verse-by-verse expository look into this supernaturally charged mystery.

Preaching the Gospel

At the top of our key passage, in verse 15, we see that it starts out pretty easy to understand. It's the Great Commission crystallized in black and white. Simply put, we are to herald the truth of the gospel. Romans 1:16 says, "I am not ashamed of the gospel of Christ: for it is the power of God unto salvation to every one that believeth." And 1 Corinthians 15:1–4 tells us what the gospel is: the death, burial, and resurrection of Jesus Christ. There's no social gospel, there's no medical gospel, and there's no civic gospel. There's only a saving gospel.

People write us letters all the time asking, "What's the magic sauce at Global Vision Bible Church?" The answer is simple: We preach the gospel—that's it! We preach the death, burial, and resurrection of Jesus Christ because Jesus is not *a* way to heaven; He is *the* only way to heaven.

I find it interesting that in Mark 16:15 Jesus tells us what to do, who to do it to, when to do it, and where to do it, but He never tells us how to do it. That's because every generation has to figure out how to effectively preach the gospel to their culture without compromising the integrity of the gospel itself. Some people use media, some people use the internet, some people use a tent, some people use a bus or even a motorcycle. Some just hoof it on foot. In the context of the full passage, Jesus just told us to use our gifts to go preach the gospel to a lost community of individuals.

While every denomination loves verse 15, many take a quantum leap over the rest of this passage as if it isn't even there. Why? Because the message makes folks uncomfortable.

The controversy starts with the front half of verse 16, which says, "He that believeth and is baptized shall be saved." Some people have problems with this for fear that it teaches baptismal regeneration, but it absolutely does not. It is the blood of Jesus Christ that washes away our sin, but baptism is an important public declaration nonetheless. In Mark 1:15 (ESV) Jesus said, "Repent and believe in the gospel," with no mention of baptism. But if you are truly saved by the grace of God, you will have no problem submitting yourself in obedience to water baptism. Your salvation is freely given to you by Jesus, and you will want to freely testify to that fact as Jesus instructs. So, baptism is a proof of your salvation, not a cause of your salvation. He clarifies that in the next phrase of our key passage: "but he that believeth not shall be damned" (Mark 16:16). He doesn't say, "He that believeth not or is not baptized." The damnation comes if you don't believe, and baptism comes because you do believe.

Everybody wants to have a gospel that's soft-served and peddled to them all nice and neat. Galatians 5:11 warns us not to take the offense out of the gospel, yet that's what we have today—churches and pastors trying to take the offense out of the cross of Christ. We want to tell you about Jesus, but we don't want to be offensive. We want to tell you about heaven, but we don't want to offend you with the prospect of hell. It's offensive to hear that you are dead, doomed, damned, and depraved, but we all need to know the hard truth so we can understand the gift of God's grace.

But God, who is rich in mercy, for his great love wherewith he loved us, even when we were dead in sins, hath quickened us together with Christ (by grace ye are saved;) and hath raised us up together, and made us sit together in heavenly places in Christ Jesus: that in the ages to come he might shew the exceeding riches of his grace in his kindness toward us through Christ Jesus. For by grace ye are saved through faith; and that not of yourselves: it is the gift of God: not of works, lest any man should boast.

—Ephesians 2:4–9

The gospel is offensive, and rightly so, because that offense is what leads you to repentance to be born again by the grace of the gospel.

They Shall Cast Out Devils

When we get to verse 17 of our key passage, we are still in the introduction of what Jesus wanted the disciples to do, as He said on the front end: "These signs shall follow them that believe…" Who are these people that believe? The same folks referenced in the previous verse, the ones who believe and get baptized because of their belief and are thereby willing to preach the gospel. He basically said to them, "Look, these things are going to happen to all who believe, and it's not going to stop."

As we continue in verse 17, we see the first of the signs that will follow all believers: "In my name shall they cast out devils." This is the key verse that established the title of this book, so please take note. Jesus said that the very first of multiple signs that will follow believers is that they shall cast out demons in His name. Jesus Himself did exactly that more than any other miraculous act during His ministry.

It empowers me to know there's still power in the name of Jesus, and there's still power in the authority of the local church, which is "the pillar and ground of the truth" (1 Tim. 3:15). The church is still God's organization, God's institution, and God's organism. It's the only entity that is infused with the power of the Holy Spirit, and Jesus said, "The gates of hell shall not prevail against it" (Matt. 16:18). If hell does not prevail, then all this nonsense in our culture will not prevail against the church of Jesus Christ, so be encouraged.

Possession or Demonization?

In the study of deliverance one of the challenges we run into is making sense of the terminology. Definitions of terms can change a lot over the course of centuries, and somewhere along the way we began to misappropriate the terms we use to identify someone who is emotionally overcome by an evil spirit. The Bible uses the words *devil*, *demon*, and *spirit* (with a lowercase *s*) interchangeably when discussing evil spirits. Meanwhile, the original Greek (that predates our modern Bibles) uses the term *demoniza* to describe those whom they attack. Yet in modern Christianity we unintentionally misuse the word *possession* because the King James version translated that word in its place (Mark 5), as has nearly every other modern Bible translation that uses the KJV as its primary source.

When we think about the word *possessed* in the context of modern English, we use the word as a condition that relates to being overcome to the point of total control or ownership. Likewise, when we consider someone overcome by an evil spirit in the context of our modern world, we immediately think of the movie *The Exorcist*. We picture someone whose flesh and soul—mind, will, and emotions—are completely and totally overcome by a demon.

The word *possessed* is in fact an unfortunate King James translation that didn't hold the same meaning back in the seventeenth century as it does now. Today the Greek word *demoniza* directly translates to the word *demonized*, not *possessed*. When we read in the King James that someone was *possessed*, our modern understanding of that word immediately has us believing there is no way this could happen to a God-fearing person. This single unfortunate reality is the cause of much of the controversy surrounding our key passage, as one confusing disconnect can easily lead to another.

> All Scripture is breathed out by God and profitable for teaching, for reproof, for correction, and for training in righteousness, that the man of God may be complete, equipped for every good work.
> —2 TIMOTHY 3:16–17, ESV

While it is true that a born-again Christian cannot be owned by a demon, they can in fact be demonized. If you're a born-again Christian, you are God's possession and cannot be possessed by anything else, but don't miss this: some have the misguided belief that because Christians cannot be possessed in modern terms, we can never be attacked or oppressed by demons—bothered and demonized in our flesh—but we absolutely can be!

Again, the word *demonized* has nothing to do with a person being *possessed* (completely overcome), but it is without question a condition that requires deliverance from one or more evil spirits. I'll be exploring this fact with great detail throughout this book.

Concerning the woman we read of in Luke 13:11 who had the *spirit of infirmity* (which is a demon), the only thing the demon attacked was the part of her body being affected by the infirmity. With the person we read of in Mark 9:25 who had the *deaf and dumb spirit*, the only part of their body that was affected was their hearing and speech. These are two examples of people who were demonized. To further clarify, demonization is the literal condition where someone can have an area of their body and/or an area of their mind under attack—afflicted, oppressed, or invaded by a devil. But praise God, Jesus said that in His name we have power to cast it out, just as He did.

> And he preached in their synagogues throughout all Galilee,
> and cast out devils.
>
> —MARK 1:39

As noted earlier, everyone wants to talk about "what would Jesus do" until it's time to do what Jesus did. The casting out of demons was something Jesus did nearly everywhere He went, the churches included (Mark 1:39). He cast out demons more than He talked about heaven and hell *combined*. Every single time He preached the gospel, the people brought those who had evil spirits, and He cast them out in His *own* name.

DISCERNING OF SPIRITS, AND DELIVERANCE

In 1 Corinthians 12 we find a list of the manifested gifts from God to the body of Christ. These spiritual gifts are given "for the perfecting of the saints, for the work of the ministry, for the edifying of the body of Christ (Eph. 4:12). I've heard pastors say there's no such thing as deliverance ministry in the Bible, but one of God's gifts to the body is the discerning of spirits, whether angelic or demonic, and the proper use of this gift is directed to the church.

Deliverance and its derivatives are indeed Bible terms that pervade the whole of Scripture, so the fact that the word *deliverance* is never found followed by the word *ministry* is irrelevant, and it's foolish to think otherwise. The words *youth* and *ministry* aren't found together in the Bible either, and no one would ever claim there is no biblical basis for such ministry.

Though the word *deliverance* is used broadly in reference to all types of spiritual freedom, the *discerning of spirits* should always involve the casting out of demons once demons are discerned. This is what we call *deliverance ministry*.

As we see in our key passage, Jesus clearly teaches that *deliverance* is the first (not the last) sign of those who believe. He said in effect, "It's all done in My name," because that's where the power is found and that's where all the glory goes.

Some people make the ministry of deliverance sound crazy, but if you stay within the confines of the Word of God, people's lives will be radically set free in the name of Jesus. No one can ever rightfully say that the power to cast out demons ever ceased, because in doing so one would be saying that the name of Jesus—and its power—is no longer available. Such a notion is nothing but heresy.

It's bewildering how people who believe that Jesus' name can save and Jesus' name can heal can also refuse to believe that there is power in Jesus' name to cast out devils. For this I challenge *all* who are reading this book: let's not live the whole of our lives and die having never done what Jesus said we must do in this regard. We are privileged to live out the text of His Great Commission—to do what Jesus did and in turn instructed us to do—and watch as it is fulfilled every day.

NEW TONGUES

As it is said, "Today, if you hear his voice, do not harden your hearts as in the rebellion."

—HEBREWS 3:15, ESV

Returning to our key passage, in my college training the phrase "they shall speak with new tongues" (Mark 16:17) was somehow whited out, redacted, and hidden from the eyes of all. Once I took off the blinders, I finally asked, "What exactly does that phrase mean?" I quickly learned that it means what the Bible said it means. The beginning of the fulfillment of that phrase is recorded in Acts 2, when the Parthians and Medes and fourteen other nationalities heard the Word of God spoken in their own language. The 120 people who gathered in the Upper Room on the day of Pentecost (Acts 1:15) were suddenly filled with the Holy Spirit and they "began to speak with other tongues, as the Spirit gave them utterance" (2:4).

Throughout the bulk of my ministry life, I tried to dismiss speaking in tongues for two reasons: 1) I was taught to do so, and 2) I'd never experienced it. I honestly thought people who practiced it were crazy. In my natural understanding, I would think the text cannot possibly mean what it says it means. But it did exactly that on the day of Pentecost, and in Paul's first letter to the Corinthians he went to great lengths to describe the difference between *speaking* and *praying* in tongues. I addressed this difference in *Accessing Your Anointing*, so I'll take a slightly different approach to discussing it here.

In reference to *speaking in tongues*, Paul concluded the passage by warning us to never forbid the speaking of tongues, rather to ensure it always flows for the edification of the church and never takes the place of prophesying (1 Cor. 14). Why? Because the Bible teaches that the person who spoke the tongue is not to be the same person who interprets the tongue (1 Cor. 14:27–28). They represent two different gifts in two different people. So, the spoken tongue leads the way to the prophetic interpretation, and the mystery of this transaction rests in the Spirit of God.

The Scripture says we must have both gifts in operation at the same time because there is to be no spoken tongue without an interpretation—God is not the author of confusion. When it is real, you'll know it's real for this reason: a true spoken tongue as a gift of the Spirit will always produce a righteous result for the edification of God's people and for the conviction of lost people. The Bible says in 1 Corinthians 14 that tongues are a sign for those who believe, and if people hear it that believe not, the prophetic interpretation of the tongue will bring them under conviction. And as we saw at Pentecost, it will bring them to Christ.

So Jesus said in effect, "Here are the signs that are going to follow the people that believe: they're going to cast out devils and speak in new languages." It's important to note that not everyone has the exact same experiences in the exact same ways. Not everybody has all the gifts or the same set of gifts. That's why they're gifts; God gives them freely to various people, for purposes of His own. He freely gives and administers the gifts of the Holy Spirit, and they're all of the same Spirit. In the body of Christ, some of us are eyes, some are hands, some are feet, some are ears, and so on.

In reference to *praying in tongues*, there is a type of prayer discussed in Romans 8 where "the Spirit himself intercedes for us with groanings too deep for words" (v. 26, ESV). Through this type of *tongue*, the Holy Spirit prays through us with verbalizations that cannot be uttered in the words of our common language, so it will indeed sound foreign to people who overhear it. We call this form of tongue our *spiritual language* or *prayer language*. I don't have to understand how it works to know that it indeed works. Jesus said it will follow those who believe, so today, in obedience, I finally flow in it; as should you, as the Holy Spirit leads.

FACING GREAT PERIL

> When you pass through the waters, I will be with you; and through the rivers, they shall not overwhelm you; when you walk through fire you shall not be burned, and the flame shall not consume you.
>
> —ISAIAH 43:2, ESV

Returning to our key passage, in the first phrase of verse 18 we read these strange words: "They shall take up serpents." This is not saying that you should walk around and pick up rattlesnakes and copperheads for no good reason. In fact, I would highly discourage you from doing something so reckless. The same is true for the promise in Isaiah 43:2 above. Just because God said He would protect us when He sends us through the fire doesn't mean we should throw ourselves into it willy-nilly. We will be protected in the face of great danger, but we shouldn't go looking for it where God doesn't lead us. Certain sects and denominations have misused this verse for a very long time, so it's understandable why so many Christians misconstrue its actual meaning.

One of the fulfillments of this promise pertaining to snakes happened in the Book of Acts when the apostle Paul was making a fire on the island of Malta. The Bible says a serpent came out from the fire and latched onto his hand (28:3). Everybody who witnessed it thought he was about to drop dead, but "Paul shook off the beast into the fire." Paul was exactly where the Lord led him, and God wasn't done with him yet, so Paul was basically snake-proof at the time. In our key verse Jesus is telling us that when things come against the people of God who are operating within His will, we should not be the least bit afraid of them.

Then, right in the middle of our key passage we read, "and if they drink any deadly thing, it shall not hurt them" (Mark 16:18). Again, God is not suggesting that we walk around drinking poison on purpose to prove how big He is. He's saying if we drink anything intended to poison us, it shall not hurt us. Today, just like then, there are people who hate the true teaching of the Word of God, and the apostles' lives were placed in jeopardy because of it. People were constantly trying to kill the early saints to silence them. And guess what? If you preach the gospel in these last of the last days, people will likewise hate you.

Jesus is telling us that we should not be afraid of the culture and the nefarious schemes to stop us from preaching the gospel. Jesus said, "You'll take up serpents, and they won't harm you, and you'll drink poison, and it won't kill you." Sadly, if you're truly following God by obeying the Great Commission, there are people who will try to destroy you just to shut you up. It happened all through church history, and it's happening to us today. But "greater is he that is in you, than he that is in the world" (1 John 4:4). "If God be for us, who can be against us?" (Rom. 8:31). "Yea, though I walk through the valley of the shadow of death, I will fear no evil: for thou art with me" (Ps. 23:4). So, fear not, children of God!

THE SICK SHALL RECOVER

Heal me, O LORD, and I shall be healed; save me, and I shall be saved: for thou art my praise.

—JEREMIAH 17:14

Then, at the end of Mark 16:18, Jesus said they (those of us who obey this passage) "shall lay hands on the sick, and they shall recover." If we believe there's power in the name of Jesus to cast out devils, then why wouldn't we believe that God can still heal people of cancer? I know He can. I've witnessed it. Is it always the will of God to heal the sick? No. Sometimes God allows sickness for purposes of His own, "that the Son of God may be glorified thereby" (John 11:4).

God can indeed use sickness in a person's life, so sometimes healing doesn't come. But don't ever use that as a cop-out. If someone asks you to pray for them, you should feel compelled to lay hands on them and pray for them right there, free of any measure of doubt no matter their condition, and fully believe that God can heal that person. Remember that our key passage of Scripture says, "These signs shall follow them that believe" (Mark 16:17), and that the laying of hands on the sick with the intent to bring healing from God is one of these signs. The power is not in our hands; it is from the Holy Spirit in the name of Jesus. We either believe that or we don't.

Shortly after we began embracing deliverance ministry, a man who has been coming to our church for many months was experiencing horrible reactions to his radiation treatments for cancer. I don't claim to have the gift of healing, but as we see in our key passage, we all have the command to speak healing over people in the name of Jesus.

One Sunday after we finished our baptismal celebrations, this man came to me and asked me to pray for him. He took off his hat, and I could see where the radiation had begun to deteriorate and scorch the skin on his head and face. Clearly aware of Hezekiah's answered prayer in the twentieth chapter of Second Kings, he then asked me to pray that God would give him fifteen more years. So I put my hand on him and started to pray.

Before starting, he asked, "Should we get down on our knees?"

I like it when people are more spiritual than the preacher. So we knelt down, and I prayed that God would heal him of cancer, restore his skin, and give him fifteen more years. Not too long ago I would have called his name out to God indirectly, asked for this man's healing, and walked away without thinking about it again. But I've watched too many people have a complete turnaround and receive full healing, so I sincerely believed for him, and I carried that belief forward with me.

The next day, the man called to tell me that after his scans that morning, the doctor informed him that the cancer was gone. "I don't have to have any more radiation," he said. "It's completely gone!"

In the time since, I have witnessed countless healing miracles in our church and on the road when I minister elsewhere—stage IV brain cancer, supposed neurological disorders; you name it, we've likely seen it with our own eyes. When I was still a cessationist, I would have sat in a church pew after hearing reports like these and been filled with doubt. I have since repented, and now I simply believe what the Bible says.

The cost of our healing was already paid by Jesus on the cross. Isaiah 53:5 says, "He was wounded for our transgressions, he was bruised for our iniquities: the chastisement of our peace was upon him; and with his stripes we are healed." The prophet Isaiah wasn't just talking about spiritual healing but all forms of healing. The Gospel of Matthew tells us that Jesus went about casting out demons and healing all who were sick, "to fulfill what was spoken by the prophet Isaiah: 'He took our illnesses and bore our diseases'" (8:16–17, ESV). As we've learned from our key passage, Jesus commissioned us to do the same. Don't ever doubt that.

THE LORD CONFIRMED IT

> So then the Lord Jesus, after he had spoken to them, was taken up into heaven and sat down at the right hand of God. And they went out and preached everywhere, while the Lord worked with them and confirmed the message by accompanying signs.
> —MARK 16:19–20, ESV

At the front end of this supernatural conclusion to the Gospel of Mark, immediately following our key passage, we are faced with two pressing questions: Do we believe in the ascension of Christ? And do we believe that He sat down at the right hand of God? Of course we do. Even cessationists passionately believe these glorious events. The only mystery that remains is found in their refusal to believe the supernatural instructions that precede these events actually mean what Jesus said they mean and still hold true today. The Great Commission as Jesus spoke it simply doesn't fit their preconceived notions, so they dismiss it.

Yet right there, immediately after Jesus gave these instructions, we see no reasons to doubt—we only see confirmations. In verse 20, Mark (an eyewitness and active participant) proves this by writing that they "went out and preached everywhere, while the Lord worked with them and confirmed the message by accompanying signs."

Don't miss the clear implications of this verse. They went out and preached the gospel just as Jesus instructed, and the signs He promised indeed followed them "while the Lord (Holy Spirit) worked with them." Jesus did not come for the miracles; He came for the message. But He used these miracles to validate the message everywhere He went, and He's still doing it today. It's not that we're looking for miracles, signs, and wonders, but the miracles, signs, and wonders are indeed confirming the supernatural nature of the gospel.

Once the gospel is preached, people get saved and their lives are forever changed. The power of the gospel that existed then is the same power of the gospel that exists right now. So the overarching question of this chapter is this: Is there still power in the name of Jesus? We either believe the Bible or we don't. We either believe Jesus or we don't.

The Theology of Experience

The body of Christ has been conditioned to a form of cultism—a half-true message that betrays the true gospel. We've been conditioned to believe and teach in a way that defies the teachings of Jesus, while in contrast, the truth of the Bible itself is crystal clear. If somehow your experience discounts the theology of Jesus, then you're missing something and it's time for a correction.

A groundswell is happening right now in the church, and this is an awakening of the highest order. Every month, every week, every day, and sometimes every hour we're watching our theology and our experience come into harmony like never before in church history. We have been commissioned to preach the gospel, to heal the brokenhearted, and to *deliver the captives* in Jesus' mighty name, so that's what we must do.

After thirty years as a preacher and evangelist, I still wonder how in the world I missed the clear truth of Mark 16 for so long—especially knowing all too well that deliverance was the number one act of Jesus after preaching the gospel. I don't understand everything we're experiencing at Global Vision Bible Church, but God has manifested Himself in so many New Testament ways that there's just no way around it. "These signs" have begun following us, and Jesus is getting all the glory.

> And they were all amazed, so that they questioned among themselves, saying, "What is this? A new teaching with authority! He commands even the unclean spirits, and they obey him." And at once his fame spread everywhere throughout all the surrounding region of Galilee.
>
> —Mark 1:27–28

Chapter 4

CAN CHRISTIANS BE DEMONIZED?

We wrestle not against flesh and blood, but against princi-
palities, against powers, against the rulers of the darkness
of this world, against spiritual wickedness in high places.

—EPHESIANS 6:12

HE CRITICS OF deliverance ministry most often point to this argument: they claim it is impossible for a born-again Christian to suffer demonic oppression, and in their estimation, they believe the Bible itself says so. The first verse these critics will point to is 1 Corinthians 6:19, which says believers are the "temple of the Holy Spirit" (ESV), which we absolutely are. But in the context of the passage we see that Paul is explicitly talking about sexual immorality and is reminding us that we should never desecrate our bodies (our temples) with perversity like fornication. Moreover, verse 19 never states that such perverse contact isn't possible for one who is indwelt with the Holy Spirit, just that it must never happen.

In verses 15–18 of 1 Corinthians 6, Paul is talking about the way we treat our bodies through idolatry and the perversity of the culture. Not one time in either of these passages does the Word of God say that a Christian cannot be under the influence of a demonic spirit. In fact, since we know that idolatry and perversity are examples of how we "wrestle" against spiritual wickedness (Ephesians 6:12 above), we see that such struggles are evidence that, without question, evil spirits can attack our minds and our bodies. In his letter to the Romans, the apostle Paul states it plainly:

> For I know that nothing good dwells in me, that is, in my flesh. For I have the desire to do what is right, but not the ability to carry it out. For I do not do the good I want, but the evil I do not want is what I keep on doing.
> —ROMANS 7:18–19, ESV

So, the man who wrote most of the books of the New Testament—the born-again, Spirit-filled man of God who taught us more about the Holy Spirit than anyone but God Himself—is clearly stating that something bad "dwells" in his flesh, and it certainly isn't of God. But it's important to see that the "nothing good" that dwells in him is not dwelling in his spirit or in his heart, but only in his flesh—in his mind and his physical body. (More on this crucial distinction later.) So, before we proceed, we must understand that in our flesh dwells no good thing, and something bad can indeed dwell there, as it did in Paul.

The Bible also says, "The works of the flesh are manifest, which are these; adultery, fornication, uncleanness, lasciviousness, idolatry..." (Gal. 5:19–20). Together this points to the fact that the Holy Spirit can live in me even as my flesh is corrupt, just as was true of Paul. If you believe a demon can't live in your flesh, you're wrong. Remember that God is omnipresent, so God's Spirit dwells with the evil of the culture, right? In fact, as David wrote under the inspiration of God, "If I make my bed in [hell], you are there!" (Ps. 139:8, ESV).

Satan is the accuser of the brethren (Rev. 12:10), and he accuses the brethren in the very throne room of almighty God, so to say that the Spirit of God and the devil cannot be in the same place at the same time is utter nonsense. When Jesus was tempted by the devil forty days and nights, they were clearly in the same place (Matt. 4:3). When Satan appealed to God and gained the right to oppress

Job, he was speaking with God in the throne room of God (Job 1:6). According to the Bible, the devil and God are in many places at the same time. The Bible is packed with proof of this simple fact.

We realize that the Holy Spirit exists wherever He wishes, regardless of the proximity of the devil, yet the argument that it's biblically impossible for a Christian to have a demon still persists. For this reason, in this chapter I will give you fifteen proofs from the Bible that a Christian can absolutely have a demon, starting with one of the most poignant examples.

1. Paul's Thorn in the Flesh

> So to keep me from becoming conceited because of the surpassing greatness of the revelations, a thorn was given me in the flesh, a messenger of Satan to harass me, to keep me from becoming conceited.
>
> —2 CORINTHIANS 12:7, ESV

Second Corinthians 12 records an unusual experience: Paul is called up to the third heaven and sees things that God won't even let him write about. He comes back and says in effect, "Because of the abundance of the revelations, I was given a thorn in my flesh," meaning in his body. Many people believe it was his eyesight, but whatever it was, it was notable. This affliction obviously bothered him because he's on record praying about it three times. Without giving us details, as we see above, Paul said the thorn in his flesh was "a messenger of Satan to harass me." The word *messenger* here is the Greek word *angelos*, which is also the word for *angel*. An angel of Satan is a demon.

Paul wrote fourteen books of the New Testament, most of which he wrote from jail, and he was closer to God than I could ever imagine being. Writing under the inspiration of the Holy Ghost, he said that a demon was harassing him and had likely given him an infirmity, and that God allowed it. If Paul could be harassed in his flesh by a demon, so can we.

2. Peter's Rebuke

In Matthew 16, after Peter rebuked Jesus for saying He must go to Jerusalem to be killed, Jesus looked at Peter and said, "Get behind me, Satan! You are a hindrance to me. For you are not setting your mind on the things of God, but on the things of man" (v. 23, ESV). Was Jesus literally calling Peter Satan? No, He was basically saying, "Peter, you are under the influence of the devil right now." Peter never would have said that otherwise. If, like Paul, Peter could be attacked by demons, so can we.

3. The Children's Bread

In Mark 7:27 (also in Matthew 15:26) Jesus calls deliverance "the children's bread." In this story, Jesus is approached by a Syro-Phoenician woman who asks Him to cast a demon out of her daughter. Jesus in effect responds, "I can't do that. It's not right for Me to cast the children's bread to the dogs." Some people would think what Jesus said to this woman was a bigoted statement, but it was meant to bring forth her faith. Jesus was simply adding emphasis to the religious divide He was about to dismiss while also setting the stage for one of the greatest acts of faith and humility recorded in the Bible.

The most common use of this verse begins by stating that Jesus is using the term "the children's bread" by focusing on the word "children" in a historical context, referring to the Jews as Abraham's seed, and that's correct. Jesus shed His blood, died, and rose again to save us all, and by doing so He broke down the middle wall of partition between Jews and Gentiles (the rest of us), so believing Gentiles are now by faith Abraham's seed as well. There is no argument about who "the children" are in this passage.

The sadly overlooked point Jesus is making here is that deliverance from demons *is* "the children's bread" in this story. The woman was asking Jesus to cast a demon out of her daughter, and Jesus clearly and immediately referred to the act as "the children's bread." While redemption and salvation are for the lost, *deliverance* is for the people of God, so the casting out of demons (the children's bread) is specifically intended for the church.

In this incredibly rich passage, it's important to note that Jesus is exposing the spirit of religion on many levels. I've come to realize that the number one demon that needs to be cast out of the church is the spirit of religion. It is the very reason why people have a hard time with deliverance ministry; they are oppressed by a religious spirit that wants to keep the entire church in bondage.

4. Ananias and Sapphira

In Acts 5, as the church abundantly grew after the day of Pentecost, we find a man named Ananias and his wife, Sapphira. This was after Pentecost, so the Holy Ghost had already fallen at this point, so this couple had been saved, filled with the Spirit, and baptized. In the context, we learn that Ananias and Sapphira sold some land and gave part of the money to the church, but obviously that wasn't the problem. The problem was they said they had given it *all*. They lied in order to look holier than thou because previously in the story (Acts 4:36–37), Barnabas (the "son of consolation") had given a large sum of money to the church and everybody responded in praise.

Ananias was saved and outwardly just as righteous as Barnabas and the rest of them. He more than likely started out well in his sincerity, but something got ahold of him. Peter provides the answer when he asks Ananias, "Why has Satan filled your heart to lie to the Holy Spirit?" (Acts 5:3, ESV). The word *filled* implies oppression—something happening from the inside. Ephesians 5:18 instructs us to "be filled with the Spirit" (the capital S always denotes the Holy Spirit), and in the account of Ananias, Peter uses the same word for "filled." So even though Ananias was filled with the Holy Ghost, he was now full of the devil. For that, he was technically speaking for the devil because he had a lying spirit in him. Peter called it out, and Ananias dropped to the floor dead, and his wife suffered the same experience three hours later.

We may be shocked that God did this, and we can be thankful He doesn't work that way every time someone lies to Him. He took this especially hard-line approach because it was the first time in the early church that division crept in through pride and deception, and God was saying, "Let Me show you what I think about division in the body of Christ." Let this be a lesson to us; God hates disunity.

5. The Ministry of Philip

Cessationists say that only the apostles cast out demons and worked miracles, yet Philip was an evangelist, not an apostle. A lot of folks mistake this Philip with the disciple Philip (one of the Twelve), but they are two different people. There are many men and women in the Book of Acts who were not apostles but nonetheless did great and mighty works and miracles. The reason why is found in our key passage from chapter 3: "These signs shall follow them that believe" (Mark 16:17). "These signs" are clearly for every child of God—all "them that believe"—and not just church leaders. This truth is inarguable. We all have the same authority that Jesus gave us in the Gospel of Mark, regardless of our place in the body.

Much of Acts 8 is about Philip encountering people who had been involved with witchcraft. When Philip came to the city of Samaria preaching Christ to them, "the people with one accord gave heed unto those things which Philip spake" (v. 6). The Bible says that when they gave heed, the crowds believed and were baptized (v. 12).

In the context, that's when Simon the sorcerer, who eventually became a false believer, saw the evident work of the Holy Spirit move in these people and wanted the same power for himself. The people were getting saved; they were getting baptized; they had heeded the ministry of the gospel that Philip was pronouncing and producing. But something happens in verse 7. After salvation came to that town, mass deliverance broke out and "unclean spirits, crying with loud voice, came out of many." Notice that this mass deliverance occurred among the same people—saved and baptized Christians—in the same context, in the same town. The devil couldn't handle this move of the Holy Spirit, so he was coming up and out in the name of Jesus immediately after the people of this town were born again.

6. The Divination Girl

Acts 16 tells the story of a girl with a spirit of divination who followed Paul and his companions for many days, calling out, "These men are the servants of the most high God, which shew unto us the way of salvation" (v. 17). One day as they headed to a prayer meeting, Paul and his companions turned around and said to the spirit, "'I command thee in the name of Jesus Christ to come out of her.' And he came out the same hour" (v. 18). The word for *divination* in the Greek is *pythonia*, which denotes a python spirit. This spirit is aptly named because it chokes the spiritual life out of people.

Was this girl telling the truth? Absolutely. You could even say she was speaking the truth prophetically. The divination spirit allows a person to flow in a prophetic gift under the wrong spirit and the wrong anointing. It is the same divination power that a fortune-teller has. I don't believe the apostle Paul would have let this girl follow him around if she were growling, foaming at the mouth, or screaming continually. She was clearly part of a group that was *following* these men of God, and in her statements she professed her faith in their message of "salvation" through Christ. She was going to Paul's prayer meetings every day, so she probably looked normal from the outside. As a slave under a spirit of divination, she was being used by her owners for profit—yet she was saying truthful things and sincerely following Paul.

When Paul finally recognized that a spirit of divination was at work in the girl, she was delivered that very hour—and Paul got arrested for it.

I want to take a brief time-out from our fifteen proofs to mention something interesting from the Old Testament concerning King Saul. The Bible says about five times that an evil spirit *from the Lord* came upon King Saul, and the only thing that would *relieve* the oppression was David playing his harp. Saul was relieved but not delivered, for there was no deliverance as we know it in the Old Testament because the authority to cast out demons was not given until Jesus walked the earth. Also, in the Psalms, we have the songs of deliverance. I've come to realize there is something powerful about having the right kind of music aiding in deliverance ministry. Likewise, there is something insidious about the wrong kind of music, as it can open demonic portals and keep you oppressed and under attack, so choose your music wisely.

The Bible says in 1 Samuel that when the evil spirit came upon Saul, he prophesied throughout the house—that is an Old Testament instance of a spirit of divination at work. The spirit of divination has not just infiltrated the church; it has in fact infiltrated the pulpit. Today we have evangelical "witch doctors" keeping people under a spell of witchcraft, falling down and worshipping at the pastors' feet, thinking they're rock-solid men of God while they're actually as crooked as a dog's hind leg. In the modern church we often see people operating with the right gift under the control of the wrong spirit. All of this underscores the importance of the discerning of spirits—deliverance ministry.

7. In My Flesh Dwells No Good Thing

In Romans 7:18 Paul says, "I know that in me (that is, in my flesh,) dwelleth no good thing." Here's the truth: *something* dwells there. If murder can be there, if rage can be there, if anger can be there, if perversion can be there and molestation can be there, then surely a demon can be there manipulating the flesh to stir these things up. It is foolish to say that all of that sin and evil can dwell in your flesh but a demon can't reside there as well. It absolutely can, and it does—even while God resides in your spirit.

As I mentioned earlier, the word *possessed* has greatly confused the church, as the original Greek word for *possession* translates to *demonization*. If you are saved by the grace of God and born again of the Spirit, the Holy Spirit resides within you, in *your spirit*. When you are demonized, the demons do not live in your spirit; they live in your flesh. So any argument that is based on the inability of a demon to live in the same place as the Holy Spirit is dashed by that reality. Demons live in our flesh, not our spirit.

Yes, we are indeed the temple of the Holy Spirit, but we have to remember that in the Bible, there was only one place in the entire temple where the presence of God dwelt: the holy of holies, where no unclean thing could go. Meanwhile, there was also an outer courtyard where even filthy animals and money changers and unbelievers could be found. Your flesh is the outer courtyard of your temple, and that's where demons can reside because in your flesh dwells no good thing!

8. The 1 Corinthians 5 Fornicator

The church of Corinth had all the gifts, but they didn't use them properly. That's why Paul wrote the letters we read as 1 and 2 Corinthians—to correct them as an apostolic father.

Paul learned that a man in the church was sleeping with his father's wife. The man was all for it, the woman was all for it, but Paul was mad about it, and he wasn't about to let that nonsense go on in the church. So Paul said, in effect, "This is wicked. Did you try to call this man to repentance?" Their modern-day response might have been, "He doesn't want to repent, so we just told him to keep it down so that he could keep on being a deacon," or, "He doesn't want to repent, so we've decided he can just stay on the prayer team." But Paul said, "Deliver this man to Satan for the destruction of the flesh, so that his spirit may be saved in the day of the Lord" (1 Cor. 5:5, ESV). Paul was saying, "This man is saved, his spirit is saved, but if he won't repent, you turn him over to the devil and let the devil have his flesh." From this we see that the devil can oppress a believer in the church.

9. Giving Place to the Devil

Ephesians 4 has a lot to do with the flesh. The works of the flesh are opposed to the things of God, but the Bible tells us how to crucify the flesh. The biblical progression for deliverance ministry is to crucify the flesh and cast out a demon—not the other way around. The Bible says when we're dealing with our flesh we put away the old man, which is deceitful according to its wicked lust (Eph. 4:22). Then we "put on the new man, which after God is created in righteousness and true holiness" (v. 24) because of the blood of Jesus.

Paul writes:

> Be ye angry, and sin not: let not the sun go down upon your wrath: Neither give place to the devil. Let him that stole steal no more: but rather let him labour, working with his hands the thing which is good, that he may have to give to him that needeth. Let no corrupt communication proceed out of your mouth, but that which is good to the use of edifying, that it may minister grace unto the hearers.
>
> —Ephesians 4:26–29

Notice that phrase "neither give place." The word *place* means occupancy, so Paul is saying don't give a foothold to the devil. In the context, he's talking about the manipulation of your flesh. So if you've done everything you can to subdue your flesh based on what the Bible says but you still have issues, that means something is manipulating your flesh from the inside out. Something is keeping you from victory. At the same time, that does not take away the occupancy of the Holy Spirit. So, what is this "place" that can be given to the devil? Clearly, it is our flesh.

10. We Wrestle Not…

In Ephesians 6:12, Paul, under the inspiration of the Holy Spirit, said, "For we wrestle not against flesh and blood." In other words, our fight is not with people; our fight is with the spirit realm: "against principalities, against powers, against the rulers of the darkness of this world, against spiritual wickedness in high places" (v. 12). We're fighting demonic activity.

A demon will overtake and oppress a good person just as it will a drunkard or a murderer. If you've opened a door somewhere legally in your life, you are in a wrestling match with the devil. In the same context Paul says, "This is what you must do to keep the devil from invading you: 'put on the whole armor of God.'" (See Ephesians 6:11–17.)

You might think that because the Bible teaches us to put on the whole armor of God, maybe we don't have to worry about demonic oppression, but it's prescriptive—a well-armored soldier still has to fight. If you don't armor up and prepare for battle, you will have to deal with demonic oppression. We all have to make a conscious effort every day to suit up.

Notice Paul's specific word choice when describing our fight. He does not simply say we fight or box or punch. He uses the word *wrestle*. Wrestling is the most hands-on form of combat there is. We are in a UFC smackdown with the devil, yet there are still people who say there's no way a Christian can have a demon when the entire point of the armor of God is to keep you from being oppressed by the enemy. I cover this subject in great detail in *Weapons of Our Warfare*, so I encourage you to read it as soon as possible.

11. The Spirit of Fear

In 2 Timothy 1:7, Paul writes, "God hath not given us the spirit of fear." When he says "us," he's talking to the church. In the context, he's like a pastor talking to his sheep. Notice he didn't call it an atmosphere or an attitude—he called it a spirit. Fear is a demonic spirit. And, as the apostle John taught us, perfect love casts out fear (1 John 4:18). So if God says to the church, "I have not given you the spirit of fear," it reveals that some people in the church indeed struggle with that spirit. That's certainly what we see with our own eyes. But as the Bible says, this spirit does not come from God. It has to come from somewhere because the text says that Christians are oppressed by it, so we know it comes from the enemy.

12. Tempted and Enticed

Another proof is found in James 1:14, where we learn, "Every man is tempted, when he is drawn away of his own lust, and enticed." In the original Greek there is only one way this phrase bears out. We already established that we have a flesh and are capable of being drawn away of our own fleshly lust. But then James adds "and enticed." The drawing away of our lust and the enticement mentioned in the text plainly come from two very different sources. Something is enticing our lust. Something is manipulating our flesh. Something is controlling our mind. If we Christians have crucified our flesh and reckoned ourselves dead, yet we still struggle with this, that's demonic oppression from the enemy.

13. Turned Aside and Taken Captive

In 1 Timothy, Paul wrote to his spiritual son, Timothy, that many of the people in the church—namely the younger widows—had "turned aside after Satan" (5:15). This tells us they were being influenced by something that had not influenced them before. Then in 2 Timothy 2:26, referring to different people but in the same context of the church, the text says they had been "taken captive" by the devil. Being *taken captive* means you are being manipulated and controlled by an outside source. These people had been taken captive by the devil and were acting according to his will.

Week after week people come to our mass deliverance services by the thousands because we don't overdramatize things. It can be said that deliverance ministry is so simple that it shouldn't work, but it works every time because it's so simple. The power is in the name of Jesus. Once you close the doors that you've opened and strip the demons' legal rights in Jesus' name, they are done! And they know they cannot stay. Yet in his letters to Timothy, Paul said there were believers who turned aside after Satan and were taken captive. These Christians chose to follow the way of error and were thereby demonized, which leads me to the next proof.

14. Giving Heed to Seducing Spirits and Doctrines of Demons

Once again writing to Timothy, Paul said, under inspiration, "Now the Spirit speaketh expressly, that in the latter times some shall depart from the faith, giving heed to seducing spirits, and doctrines of devils" (1 Tim. 4:1). He isn't warning us about what the godless culture is going to do. We already know that the culture is on a collision course with destruction. We also know we can't follow Jesus and the culture at the same time—it's impossible. "A double-minded man is unstable in all his ways" (Jas. 1:8). So this isn't a warning to the world; it's for the church.

Paul is warning us that in the last days God's people will give heed to and be seduced by demonic spirits. It's hard to give heed to something that isn't talking to you, and anything that can talk is a person (in this case, a demon). These people will not only give heed to seducing spirits but will also begin to give heed to demonic doctrines. From this we see that once you listen to a demonic doctrine, you start to give in to demons.

When I went through deliverance, one of the things I had to deal with was the religious spirit that had oppressed me for most of my life. Religious spirits have been around a very long time. Religious spirits caused the people to crucify Jesus. The people didn't kill Jesus because of what He did; they killed Him because of what He said. "No one ever spoke like this man!" (John 7:46, ESV). The one thing the religious spirits hated more than anything else was the fact that Jesus had power and authority over them. When He used that authority, they called Him a heretic.

Take note that demons today still respond to Jesus the exact same way they did when He walked the earth. Likewise, religious people today respond to deliverance the same way they did when Jesus did it in His day. Even though deliverance sets desperate people free, it still makes religious people angry because they're giving heed to doctrines of demons.

15. The Testimony of Those Delivered

For the final proof in my review (which is in no way exhaustive) I have *experience* as the basis. During a debate we held about deliverance, the opposing side said we were basing our stance solely on experience. My response was that believers base their salvation on experience. Think about it: one of the reasons you *know* you're saved is because you bring forth good fruit. "Old things are passed away; behold, all things are become new" (2 Cor. 5:17). It's not just walk an aisle, sign a card, and pray a prayer. There's evidence in your life. There's a change in your life. The manifest presence of God changes you from who you were to who you are today. You know you are saved because 1) the Bible says so and 2) God changed your life. That's *experience-based theology.*

This fifteenth and final proof is simply the testimony of those delivered throughout Scripture, history, and the church today. If you want to prove that Christians experience demonic oppression and can be released from it by the power of Jesus' name, all you need is the testimony of those who have been set free. Ask any of the tens of thousands of born-again Christians who have been delivered from demons in our ministry alone—myself, Tai, our staff, and all our deliverance team included—and you'll know. We all want complete freedom and healing and the fullness of all the Lord has promised, so we simply take Jesus at His word to do what Jesus did, and now we testify. In the end, when our final deliverance is at hand and we conquer the accuser once and for all, our testimony will prove second only to the blood of Jesus as evidence of our victory.

> Come and hear, all you who fear God, and I will tell what he
> has done for my soul. I cried to him with my mouth, and high
> praise was on my tongue. If I had cherished iniquity in my

heart, the Lord would not have listened. But truly God has listened; he has attended to the voice of my prayer.

—PSALM 66:16–19, ESV

Chapter 5

NINE (RIDICULOUS) OBJECTIONS TO DELIVERANCE MINISTRY

So also faith by itself, if it does not have works, is dead. But someone will say, "You have faith and I have works." Show me your faith apart from your works, and I will show you my faith by my works. You believe that God is one; you do well. Even the demons believe—and shudder!

—JAMES 2:17–19, ESV

EVER SINCE GLOBAL Vision Bible Church started operating in the supernatural gifts of the Holy Spirit, and especially deliverance ministry, we've learned to deal with endless criticism and pushback from the religious crowd. I've heard countless ridiculous objections, and in this chapter I'm going to let the Bible dismiss the nine most common of these. While I know this will serve you well in painting a clear biblical picture to settle the debate, I've learned that at the end of the day, the people who don't understand deliverance are the people who don't want to understand deliverance.

Many of those who reject deliverance ministry have seen it abused in the church, so I get it. As disappointing as this can be, there are also people who pervert the gospel in the church, but that doesn't mean we stop preaching it, right? The fact that some people are doing deliverance improperly is not an excuse for rejecting Jesus' instruction to cast out demons. Why? Because we're commanded to do it. We're commissioned to do it. We have been given authority and the anointing to do it, and the body of Christ desperately needs it. We are in the ministry for the freedom of others, not for the approval of others, so we all have to make up our minds whether we're going to please people or please God—whether we're going to pursue our own comfort or pursue the things of God. So let's put aside our excuses long enough to properly discern His will in this matter.

Ridiculous Objection 1: Deliverance Is Not in the Bible

This first objection is utter nonsense, but I hear it all the time, so let's dismiss it now. If you search for the word *deliver* or *deliverance* or even *delivering* in the Bible, you will see it's there repeatedly—perhaps not in the same immediate context, but even the Book of Psalms contains numerous songs of such deliverance. When an evil spirit from the Lord came upon Saul, the song from David's harp temporarily delivered him from this oppression. So David began to produce songs of deliverance. In the journey out of Egypt, the people of God were oppressed and brought forth out of Egyptian bondage because they needed deliverance.

Deliverance from evil is a fundamental concept in the Bible. In Luke 4:18, quoting Isaiah 61:1–2, Jesus said, "The Spirit of the Lord is upon me, because he hath anointed me to preach the gospel to the poor; he hath sent me to heal the brokenhearted, to preach *deliverance to the captives*" (emphasis added). At some point over the past two thousand years people under the influence of the spirit of religion began to claim that deliverance is not a concept we need to deal with in the ways that Jesus taught us to deal with it, so some began to use this form of wordplay to make the ridiculous claim that it's not in the Bible—even though it's mentioned in literally every book throughout the Word of God.

How can we not see this as the scarlet thread of theology through the entirety of the Old and New Testaments? While God has to mention deliverance only once to make it biblical, He mentioned it hundreds of times. In the Gospels of Matthew, Mark, Luke, and John alone, deliverance is mentioned in 286 verses, all dealing with evil spirits being cast out.

Deliverance makes up a third of what Jesus did in His ministry. In fact, outside of preaching the gospel, it's the number one thing Jesus did. Acts 10:38 summarizes Jesus' ministry by stating, He "went about doing good, and healing all that were oppressed of the devil." In that context, we're reminded that sickness is often a direct result of demonization, and in many of Jesus' deliverances recorded in the Gospels, Jesus also healed the person immediately after casting out his or her demons. No matter what you want to call it, the Bible commands it.

> You yourselves know what happened throughout all Judea, beginning from Galilee after the baptism that John proclaimed: how God anointed Jesus of Nazareth with the Holy Spirit and with power. He went about doing good and healing all who were oppressed by the devil, for God was with him.
> —ACTS 10:37–38, ESV

Ridiculous Objection 2: Deliverance Was Only for Jesus to Do

After being a cessationist for thirty years, I've often felt the need to publicly repent in humiliation and say, "I simply missed it." The Great Commission as recorded in Mark 16 is one of the passages that eluded me all that time. When Jesus said, "And these signs shall follow them that believe; in my name shall they cast out devils" (Mark 16:17), He was plainly talking to *all* believers, us included, and I missed that—not out of ignorance but because I was taught in seminary that "these signs" that follow only applied to Jesus and the disciples *during Jesus' ministry* on earth. But if signs and wonders—including the casting out of evil spirits—were only to be performed up until the end of His ministry, then why did Jesus wait until the end of His ministry to say this and give the commission? After all, the word *shall* never refers to the past, and He clearly states that "these signs *shall* follow them that believe."

Within seconds of delivering this commission, Jesus ascended into heaven and sat down at the right hand of God to make intercession for you and me. It's foolish to believe that Jesus would commission His disciples to start their ministry with these promises of miraculous power only to end it before they could get started. Yet there are people who actually teach this, as if Jesus was saying, "Now, this is what I want you to do, but you've only got about fifteen seconds to do it because I'm going back to heaven, and it only applies to you while I'm still here!"

Jesus was *not* saying the ministry that would be followed by "these signs" would end when He left. He was saying it was just getting geared up. He said, in effect, "Go to Jerusalem and wait in the Upper Room until you are filled with the power of the Holy Spirit from on high. Then, when you get that infilling, Peter, you go out and preach!" From there the Spirit of God fell and three thousand people got saved and baptized, which is just the first of an uncountable number of proofs that "these signs" and wonders were just beginning to follow "those who believe."

The church is here today because of what happened on the day of Pentecost. God said in Joel 2:28, "I will pour out my spirit upon all flesh." It started on that day, and it is still going to this day. If you don't believe that, you were never taught to read the Bible correctly.

Ridiculous Objection 3: After Jesus, Deliverance Was Only for the Apostles

The next ridiculous thing people say is "Signs and wonders were only for the twelve apostles." The only problem with that is in Luke 10, Jesus ordained seventy, over and above the Twelve, to do exactly what they were doing, and they did it. "And the seventy returned again with joy, saying, Lord, even the devils are subject unto us through thy name" (v. 17). That should settle that.

But then an alternate objection emerges: "It was just for these two groups combined; they're the only ones that had this power." But the Gospels tell us of a time when the apostle John said to Jesus, "'Master, we saw someone casting out demons in your name, and we tried to stop him, because he does not follow with us.' But Jesus said to him, 'Do not stop him, for the one who is not against you is for you'" (Luke 9:49–50, ESV). This clearly tells us this unknown deliverance minister was not one of the Twelve, nor one of the seventy.

Some critics extend this objection to include just the apostle Paul in this group that had the power to cast out demons, believing it all ended with him. But the Bible tells us about a man named Philip, who was not an apostle but a deacon in the church, who cast out devils and performed miracles (Acts 8:5–7). We commonly call him Philip the evangelist, not to be confused with the apostle Philip, who was one of the original Twelve.

And then there was Stephen, who was also a deacon in the church and became the first martyr. Here's what the Bible says about him: "And Stephen, full of faith and power, did great wonders and miracles among the people" (Acts 6:8). Next we read about Barnabas, who also wasn't an apostle, yet he was doing miracles. And there was Silas, who also wasn't an apostle, and he too was doing miracles. So the argument that only the apostles had that power falls apart once you actually read the Bible!

It's also important to note that church history is filled with people who believed signs and wonders were meant to be a part of the church's ministry long after the apostles died, and that included the casting out of demons.

Ridiculous Objection 4: It's Not an Important Issue

The fourth objection to deliverance ministry is that it's not important. If being a recurring and emphatic pattern of the New Testament church isn't enough to make it important, then nothing is important. If delivering people from evil isn't important to the church, then what is?

Some critics claim that deliverance ministry is unimportant because all the demons in the world were already cast out by Jesus, the apostles, and other first-century Christians. To that I ask, "When they were cast out, where did they all go?" Scripture tells us they won't be cast into the lake of fire until the very end, so today they're still doing what they've always done. For that, there's only one way to deal with them, and it's as important an issue today as it was then: we must cast them out in the mighty name of Jesus Christ.

To say deliverance ministry is not important or that the Bible doesn't emphasize it is to ignore and dismiss verse after verse and story after story intended to instruct us. As I will continue to remind us, Jesus included it in the Great Commission as a commandment, not a suggestion (Mark 16:17). Every single documented encounter Jesus had with demons should encourage us. We still have power to cast them out and see them respond with terror the same way they did when He walked the earth. In contrast, what is *not* important is all the superfluous, non-biblical nonsense we see emphasized in most churches in America today.

When I visit churches, nine times out of ten their baptistery is full of Christmas decorations. They haven't baptized converts in weeks, months, or sometimes even years. The plain truth is we emphasize buildings, parking lots, and programs that celebrate how wonderful we are, and none of it has any sustainability or lasting fruit. God doesn't care what our buildings look like, but He clearly wants the church to armor up and stand against the devil's schemes (Eph. 6:11) and fight the good fight of the faith (1 Tim. 6:12). How much time does the church spend engaged in actual spiritual warfare?

The church in America is trying to preach people happy, telling them they're going to have "life and life more abundantly" only to send them back home addicted to pornography, prescription medications, and other lusts of the flesh. We preach these cotton-candy sermons but then turn around and say, "We're not going to discuss the casting out of evil spirits because that would be heresy." It's no coincidence that the first time Jesus cast out a demon, they called Him worse than a heretic. They said, "You cast out devils by the prince of the devils." (See Matthew 9:34, ESV.) Meanwhile, Jesus issued the severest of warnings to all who would attribute the power of the Holy Spirit to Satan (specifically in reference to the casting out of demons; Matthew 12:22–32), so it's clearly of the utmost importance to Him.

We often hear people say we're going overboard at Global Vision, and that all we ever do is talk about fighting demons and deliverance. While it's obviously not *all* we ever talk about, it is definitely a huge point of emphasis for us. After thirty years in the ministry, we're finally taking authority in Jesus' name, and it's better late than never.

Now that God has removed the scales from my eyes, how can I *not* emphasize what He has revealed to me? How can I not tell the truth about deliverance and true spiritual warfare now that I know it?

Jesus has commissioned the church to walk on the front line of this war, not to act as if the enemy doesn't even exist. We've done that for far too long. Look around and see the results of our ignorance. In these last of the last days, the enemy is already within the gates, so deliverance is of the highest importance.

> Finally, my brethren, be strong in the Lord, and in the power of his might. Put on the whole armour of God, that ye may be able to stand against the wiles of the devil. For we wrestle not against flesh and blood, but against principalities, against

powers, against the rulers of the darkness of this world, against spiritual wickedness in high places.

—EPHESIANS 6:10–12

Ridiculous Objection 5: Deliverance Is a Charismatic Practice

The fifth objection is that deliverance is only a Charismatic practice. We already know that deliverance is found everywhere in the Bible, so how could it only be for Charismatics? This bigoted objection is clearly rooted in the spirit of religion; yet let me share something I find very interesting. If you go back in history (and our seminaries won't tell us this for some reason), there were Baptists, Methodists, Wesleyans, and churches in every denomination you can name that believed in deliverance ministry. Even the great reformer Martin Luther battled the devil head-on. Luther would never be mistaken for a Charismatic. If you go to his office, you'll see an ink spot on the floor where he picked up an ink bottle, threw it at the devil, and told the devil to get out of his office. He wrote about it and often talked about the demonic (what would have been called *exorcism* in his day). Jonathan Edwards—a key leader in the Great Awakening of the 1700s and the author of *Sinners in the Hands of an Angry God*—preached about demonic influence in people's lives.

Win Worley was a strict Southern Baptist who got baptized in the Holy Spirit and simply fell into deliverance ministry. He was so far ahead of his time that people didn't know what to do with it. Though he's been with the Lord for many years, his church still holds an annual deliverance conference. The church needs to stop labeling things as *unbiblical* that are clearly in the Bible, as only the enemy could be behind such ignorant deception.

While we're on the subject of Charismatics who practice biblical deliverance, if you're critical of them just because you don't understand them or don't like who they follow, you need correction. Jesus addressed this issue when John made a similar complaint. Don't miss this: deliverance ministry has the power to unify the church. Just ask Jesus:

> John said to him, "Teacher, we saw someone casting out demons in your name, and we tried to stop him, because he was not following us." But Jesus said, "Do not stop him, for no one who does a mighty work in my name will be able soon afterward to speak evil of me. For the one who is not against us is for us."
>
> —MARK 9:38–40, ESV

Ridiculous Objection 6: It's Dangerous to Talk About Demons

This sixth objection is beyond ridiculous, as it can have devastating results. People are afraid to talk about demons because they fear they'll get them stirred up. Of course you'll get them stirred up; they've been comfortably in charge for long enough. In deliverance ministry, we're absolutely trying to stir them up to get them up and out! If you had a home invader hiding in your garage fully intending to take you captive and steal from you, would you be hesitant to call the police for fear of upsetting them? This sort of fear is common, but it's wrong. It's straight from the demons that oppress us. Once you truly realize you have full power to safely remove these demons and to permanently remove their legal right to ever return, that fear should be gone. So fear not!

Assuming these critics are believers, I want to ask them a few questions: Do you not believe in the power and authority of the name of Jesus? Do you not believe in the covering of the blood of Jesus? For years I thought it was an unscriptural practice to give credence to or recognize the power of demons. Then suddenly I realized that everywhere Jesus went, the people started manifesting evil spirits, and He didn't respond by saying, "You unscriptural, nonsensical individual; you couldn't just wait until after church?" Or "Stop getting stirred up, demon! You're upsetting the peace of the church service, and you're scaring the people!" No. Jesus immediately dealt with it. He immediately spoke to the demon and called it out. Stirring up demons never embarrassed Him. It never stopped Him. And it certainly never worried Him or scared Him.

When you finally witness someone experience deliverance in your church, you will never again have to convince the congregation that there are real, evil spirits dwelling in the flesh of Christians that need to be cast out. As the church, we need to break the fear that keeps us from boldly doing what Jesus did, especially when it's something He commissioned every believer to do. When we cast out a demon in Jesus' name and by His authority, it is the demon who will tremble with fear, not the believer. So fear not—God is with us (Isa. 41:10)!

Ridiculous Objection 7: Deliverance Should Never Be Practiced Publicly

Jesus delivered people publicly—out in the open with witnesses—even in the church house. The Gospel of Mark tells us from the very beginning that Jesus "preached in their synagogues throughout all Galilee, and cast out devils" (Mark 1:39). He literally went from town to town and synagogue to synagogue, casting out evil spirits everywhere He went. The first chapter of Mark is a fascinating study of how Jesus first made His presence known by publicly delivering people from demons, and it wasn't just one or two times. Mark tells us that shortly after battling Satan in the wilderness, Jesus' first public demonstration of power was to deliver a man from a demon in the synagogue, after which He ministered to "all the city" well into the night as He "cast out many devils" (vv. 33–34). When the Holy Ghost goes out of His way to say He delivered "many" with "all the city" present, He means *many*. He doesn't mean just a handful, and it wasn't done in private.

As we study the way Jesus cast out demons, it's evident that witnesses were not only welcome, but they were the norm, as their testimonies played a direct role in bringing attention to the ministry of Jesus (vv. 27–28). When God repeats Himself or draws expressive illustrations to describe something, we should always take notice that He is making an emphatic point. Jesus continued this pattern everywhere He went, and so should we.

I find it especially interesting that deliverance always started up in the synagogues. These people were not wicked, deviant, crack-smoking lunatics. They were sitting in a church service submitting themselves to spiritual authority and sound doctrine. But when the Word came out of Jesus, the demons started manifesting in the congregation and Jesus just cast them out. Don't miss that. Jesus didn't hesitate—He immediately cast the spirit out of the man and left the man in the synagogue. If a demon manifested in a man like that today, the average church would kick the man out of the church and leave the demon in the man.

There's a lot of conjecture about how we should go about deliverance, but it isn't about methodology. It's about the message of the power of Jesus' name. It's about the anointing and the authority God's people have been commissioned to walk in. The Bible shows us many different ways to deliver people from evil spirits. For that, each of the deliverance ministers we introduce in *Come Out in Jesus Name* approaches deliverance in a slightly different way. I've witnessed more approaches to deliverance ministry than I can list here. But I refuse to let this book become a guide to a particular set of methodologies. Each of these approaches works because the power isn't in the methodology or the minister, but only in the name of Jesus and the Holy Spirit working in us and through us.

My desire is for those in the ministry—pastors, preachers, and other church leaders—to think about the scenario of someone suddenly manifesting a demon in the church and just let it sink in, because it's going to happen eventually. In fact, I suggest you start praying that it happens sooner than later. Think about the context of your church on a Sunday morning and how a service currently flows. Imagine the preaching and the relative quiet, and then imagine somebody suddenly standing up with an unnerving, demonic scream. What would your response be? What would the people's response be? Contrast that to what Jesus and the disciples would have done in this scenario. Your church needs to close that gap, and fast.

If the church leaders will simply act without hesitation to call out the evil spirit in Jesus' name, an oppressed soul will be set free, a church will be forever changed, and God will get the glory. Leaders, your people are going to follow your lead when you act in the authority of Jesus. Sure, you can choose to stand there like a deer in the headlights and wonder to yourself what you are going to do next. You can cut the live feed. You can get five deacons to drag the person out before they cause any more embarrassment. But I pray you will choose to show forth the manifest presence and the "finger of God" right there in that service (Luke 11:20).

If you're a pastor, I exhort you to come down from that platform, walk right up to that demonized individual, and say to that evil spirit, "In the name of Jesus, I command you to release her. Come up and out right now!" Do that, and the Holy Spirit will light your church on fire! People will start telling their friends and neighbors, and the thing you thought would scare them will be the very thing that brings revival to your church. You are both shepherd and watchman, and your congregation needs you to lead.

> Be sober-minded; be watchful. Your adversary the devil prowls around like a roaring lion, seeking someone to devour. Resist him, firm in your faith, knowing that the same kinds of suffering are being experienced by your brotherhood throughout the world.
>
> —1 PETER 5:8–9, ESV

Ridiculous Objection 8: Not Every Problem Is a Demon

I can't tell you how many times I've heard this one. I get it, and it's true (much more on this subject later), but that's just another cop-out people use to avoid having to mess with demons. It's said that not every sickness is demonic, but what would be the harm if we were to take authority over every sickness as if it were and see how many more people get healed in our churches than have been for the last few years? As we see over and over in the New Testament (see Acts 10:38 above), Jesus often cast out demons before healing the people, so there is a clear connection between the two miracles. If an ailment is demonic, then deliverance can bring healing. If it is not, then there's no harm done. The effort to cast out evil spirits can only help the person.

I think some of us hesitate because we're afraid someone might walk in asking for healing, and doubt or the fear of failure creeps in, so at best we might pray for them but never truly believe we have the authority to actually initiate their healing. For that we fail to boldly call out any evil spirits, and we certainly don't exhibit any faith that the person will be healed. Instead anxiety overtakes us and we feel powerless. The enemy is counting on this; that's why he sowed this sort of confusion into our theology.

Take note of this: the Bible doesn't say that Jesus went around *praying* for healing; it says He went around *healing* and casting out demons—including the spirit of infirmity.

We lay hands on people, anoint them, and pray for them because the Bible tells us to do so (Jas. 5:14), and we fully expect the people to be healed. We cast out demons for the same exact reason, through the same exact power. This is the power of the supernatural realm that is all around us, and it's the same power that the original disciples displayed when they were commissioned to do so. The same should be true of us.

> And they went out, and preached that men should repent.
> And they cast out many devils, and anointed with oil many
> that were sick, and healed them.
>
> —MARK 6:12–13

There is absolutely no harm in going through proper deliverance regardless of your condition, so those with infirmities should definitely seek it. A famous battle cry among established deliverance ministers is "When in doubt, cast it out!" And they're right.

Ridiculous Objection 9: Deliverance Makes People Uncomfortable

The ninth objection can't find a shred of basis anywhere in the Bible, yet it's the most common gripe we hear. We can't even talk about deliverance ministry without seeing people squirm. Somehow the word *deliverance* sounds strange to folks. There was a minor revival of deliverance ministry a while back, but the church eventually put a lid on it. We put it back under a cloak of darkness because people were simply afraid of it. I believe the reason people get so uncomfortable with the subject is because it convicts them. Deep inside they know it was a massive part of Jesus' ministry, so all the years of ignoring it doesn't sit well with our pride.

It really is amazing to realize that the number one objection to deliverance is the fact that it freaks people out. Well, of course it does! We're talking about casting out demons—the supernatural enemies of God and the most threatening enemies of humanity. They hate us, and they want to destroy us.

We are made in God's image, and the devil can't stand that. Revelation 12 says, "Woe to the inhabiters of the earth and of the sea! for the devil is come down unto you, having great wrath, because he knoweth that he hath but a short time" (v. 12). Why is the devil so angry? Because he knows he's going to hell very soon, and he's doing everything he can to take as many people with him as possible (John 10:10). For this, we have no choice but to make people uncomfortable. Satan is real. Demons are real. Hell is real. There's a war raging for the souls of men, and the great and terrible day of the Lord is drawing near (Joel 2:31).

This isn't about who has the biggest church, who has the most programs, or who has the most followers on social media. We don't have time to worry about popularity or numbers games. God isn't impressed, and neither is the devil. The only thing demons care about is stopping you from walking in the authority the Bible says you have. When God honors His Word through the act of deliverance, people will take notice. When they realize there's a place where they can end the suffering in their flesh and simply feel loved for who they are, they'll awaken from the slumber of lifeless religion and church as usual. They won't care about comfort anymore. They'll just want freedom.

> Besides this you know the time, that the hour has come for you to wake from sleep. For salvation is nearer to us now than when we first believed. The night is far gone; the day is at hand. So then let us cast off the works of darkness and put on the armor of light.
>
> —ROMANS 13:11–12, ESV

PART 2

JESUS ON DELIVERANCE

Chapter 6

WHEN KINGDOMS COLLIDE

If a son shall ask bread of any of you that is a father, will he give him a stone? or if he ask a fish, will he for a fish give him a serpent? Or if he shall ask an egg, will he offer him a scorpion? If ye then, being evil, know how to give good gifts unto your children: how much more shall your heavenly Father give the Holy Spirit to them that ask him?

—LUKE 11:11–13

I N THIS CHAPTER we're going to take a deeper look into the early days of Jesus' ministry by studying a key passage in Luke 11. Starting with the verses above, we see Jesus gave us one of the most important principles of the Bible, and He made it plain. He said, "If you want more from God, ask the Father for the indwelling and empowerment of the Holy Spirit." Jesus had a way of talking real to people. He said, "I know you're evil, but if your son or daughter comes to you and says, 'I want an egg,' are you going to say, 'Oh, OK, let me give you a scorpion'?"

When the people heard Jesus ask this set-up question, it was laughably offensive—but that was the point. Jesus was trying to get them to understand how ridiculous it is to miss the fullness of all the Father wants for us. If your son wants bread, you don't give him a rock instead. Can you imagine having that sort of back-and-forth with your child? "Daddy, I'm hungry. I need a snack." You respond, "Why don't you go out back and chew on a piece of gravel, son." Jesus was being purposefully abrasive to make a point that no one would forget. When we need deliverance and healing, the Lord won't give us dead religion as the church gives it.

Jesus was offensive on purpose because the gospel is offensive. The offense leads to conviction, and conviction leads to redemption. If you think you've got it all together, you won't believe you need God. But when God stomps your religion into the ground and offends you with the truth that you need Jesus, it will motivate you to righteousness. You'll know that He's the one and only way you'll change. Do not fall into the denominational mindset that Jesus was always sweet, meek, and mild, or that He never said anything to hurt anyone's feelings. On the contrary, most of what Jesus said was intended to leave a mark.

THERE IS MORE

"If ye then, being evil, know how to give good gifts unto your children: how much more...?" (Luke 11:13). Beloved, God has so much more for us than we've been experiencing in modern Christianity that it's ridiculous! The body of Christ is more than just gathering at 10:30 sharp on a Sunday morning and getting out at 12:00 dull. We know when to stand, and we know when to sit. We know when to sing, and we know when to shut up. We don't schedule too many baptisms because we don't want to go too long. We know when to say "oh me," and we know when to say "amen." In the American church, we are careful not to let things break out. We are careful not to invite the Holy Spirit to do what only He can do.

I've got to be honest; we were that way at Global Vision for a very long time. When you're shepherding people, you can tell when God is getting ready to break loose with something, and on many occasions over the years I could feel it rising. Sadly, whenever that happened, I would squelch the music a little bit and tamp everybody back down to normal because I knew if I let it flow freely, something uncomfortable would happen—something I was trained to quench would break out. Now I just take the lid off and let it happen!

Jesus said to the lukewarm church of Laodicea, "I'll spew you out of My mouth." (See Revelation 3:16.) If the lukewarm church makes Jesus so sick He wants to vomit them out, you can be sure He's not showing up on Sunday morning. The presence of Jesus does not invade the average church in this nation because they have been taught that religion and social programs are all there is. The Bible has been prodding us for a very long time. There is much more to the kingdom of God—there is much more to the Holy Spirit than we've been taught by men.

RELIGION'S RESPONSE TO AUTHORITY

Luke chapter 11 records a very busy time in the ministry of Jesus. For three and a half years He was always working, but the pace of His ministry was accentuated at times, and this is one of those times. He had been preaching the Sermon on the Mount, casting out devils, rebuking the Pharisees, and going from synagogue to synagogue preaching the gospel of the kingdom. He stayed up all night ministering to people who had spirits of infirmity. He prayed for the sick, healed the lepers, raised the dead, walked on water, and fed multitudes with hush puppies and sardines.

Everywhere Jesus went, people wanted Him to lay His hands upon them. He caused such a stir that the very things He preached—including being set free through deliverance—did two things: they brought Him the most criticism, and they gave Him the most fame. Jesus' radical ministry drove the common people to Him, and it drove away the religious people who could not stand the truth of the gospel. The same thing is true today. Preaching the full truth of the gospel will draw the hearts of the hungry and repel the hearts of the religious.

I thank God for my Christian upbringing and how my college and seminary taught me to love the Bible, but a time came when I had to take God out of the powerless denominational box. I finally had to open the Bible and read it anew while asking the Holy Spirit alone to teach me. My wife, Tai, never had to overcome religion. Her seminary involved climbing out of a ditch of addiction and falling into her secret place of intimacy with God. She's one of those people whose first honest reading of the Bible (and every reading thereafter) was led by the Holy Spirit alone, so no human teacher messed her up with man-made doctrines.

When we discussed Scripture early on in our marriage, I envied Tai's literal view of the Word of God and her unadulterated understanding of the supernatural workings of the Holy Spirit. Years later, her growing passion for these helped start me on this journey out of dead religion. I committed myself to reading the Bible with fresh eyes, to fast with genuine spiritual intent, and to pray until I received the answers because I knew there was more to God than I had been told. Our key passage from Luke tells us there is much more to God than we have been taught, and we should ask for it.

Now that God has answered, there is no going back; we simply know too much. God has opened the box, and we are not stuffing Him back in. We're going to set this nation on fire with the truth and the power of the Holy Spirit. This is our commission. To go back now would be rebellion and disobedience to the clear teachings of the Word of God.

> And he was casting out a devil, and it was dumb. And it came
> to pass, when the devil was gone out, the dumb spake; and
> the people wondered. But some of them said, He casteth out
> devils through Beelzebub the chief of the devils. And others,
> tempting him, sought of him a sign from heaven.
> —LUKE 11:14–16

Returning to our key passage, after Jesus tells the people there is more through the power of the Holy Spirit, the very next phrase says, "And he was casting out a devil" (v. 14). Notice how casual that transition was. He flowed from preaching the power of the Holy Spirit to casting out a devil. Other Bible translations say, "Now he was casting out a demon" (ESV), so it's important to realize the immediacy of the teaching and the act. Verse 14 continues, "When the devil was gone out, the dumb spake; and the people wondered." In modern vernacular that means they marveled; they were flabbergasted and were thinking, "What in the world just happened?" This man could not speak, and probably hadn't spoken in his entire life, yet when Jesus cast a mute spirit out of him, the man immediately began to speak. It was a clear miracle from God to them, and people still have the same response of shock and wonder when they see demons leave a person today. As commonplace as it should be, it is still a miracle from God, and we should never minimize that.

Now, here's the shocking part of our key passage. Some of the religious people who witnessed this miracle said Jesus was casting out devils through the power of Beelzebub (v. 15). The name Beelzebub means "lord of the flies," which is the prince of the devils. The terrible error we see in the religious people then is the same thing we see in most church people today. They believe they have all kinds of knowledge about the devil but have no knowledge of how to deal with him. We will revisit this incredibly rich (and blasphemous) confrontation between the Pharisees and Jesus later in this book. It's so incredibly rich with revelation that it will take more than one chapter to explore it, so hold on to your hat if you're hungry for a deeper look.

Most people who deny the power of deliverance ministry do not deny the existence of demons. They just deny the fact that we have been commissioned with authority over them. That's how the religious spirit has crept into the churches in America and around the world, and it happened the same way in the Bible. The religious people who confronted Jesus had a theological concept of the devil but no understanding of what to do with him. But the people of God who understand and obey the Bible know what to do with him: "Submit yourselves therefore to God. Resist the devil, and he will flee from you" (Jas. 4:7). We must submit to the Word of God and actively reject the demons.

If you don't learn how to effectively fight the enemy, you will end up fighting the people who fight the enemy, just as these religious folks fought against Jesus in our passage. The people, in effect, said, "This isn't real—this is hocus-pocus witchcraft. He's doing this by the prince of devils." Then, in verse 16 we see, "And others, tempting him, sought of him a sign from heaven." Isn't that just like religious people? They just saw a sign! They had just experienced a miracle, but all they could do was rationalize it away in attempt to strip the power from the gospel. That's religion for you. The truth is we're not ever seeking signs, but as Jesus promised in Mark 16:17, the signs are seeking after us. Signs and wonders will always follow the truth of the gospel!

A HOUSE DIVIDED

> But he, knowing their thoughts, said unto them, Every kingdom divided against itself is brought to desolation; and a house divided against a house falleth.
>
> —LUKE 11:17

After Jesus cast out the spirit from the mute man, in verse 16 the religious people basically asked Him to prove that He was valid—that He really had power from the living God. So, through His famous words recorded in verse 17 above, Jesus immediately validated both the kingdom of God and the kingdom of Satan. In His loaded metaphorical fashion, He made the point that while God indeed has a kingdom of supernatural power, the devil also has a supernatural kingdom—and it is a very well-ordered, strategically structured kingdom. Can you guess where the devil learned this sophisticated organizational structure? In heaven with God. When Satan fell, along with the angels who rebelled with him (see Ezekiel 28; Isaiah 14; Matthew 12–13), he took the rank-and-file administration that God had so sovereignly and perfectly placed in heaven.

It's important to know that the devil can't create anything; instead, he has to steal or imitate what God has already created. That's why he's called an antichrist spirit.

Jesus says point-blank that the devil has a kingdom, and it's not a ragtag bunch of ghostly figures haunting abandoned houses or roaming around like brainless zombies. It's a well-oiled military machine with principalities, powers, rulers, and plans of spiritual wickedness working from high places (Eph. 6:12). Satan controls literal structured principalities over certain regions and holds power over certain governments. That's why some areas of this nation and around the world have a dark cloud of perversion and wickedness over them—a shroud of rebellion and witchcraft manipulating them. The Bible reminds us that we wrestle not against flesh and blood but against those principalities and powers; not against the men and women running the governments but against the administration of demons controlling them through their flesh. And a sophisticated administration it is.

By now, most folks realize Jesus' famous statement that "Every kingdom divided against itself is brought to desolation" (Matt. 12:25) is true regardless of the government or scope. Julius Caesar built the Roman Empire to horrific dominance on this all-powerful axiom—divide and conquer. It's an absolute truth that was well known among the people of Jesus' time. So, when these religious people accused Jesus of throwing out the devil by the power of the devil, He easily rebuked them with this now famous verse, a verse so profoundly relevant to this nation that Abraham Lincoln used it in his famous "House Divided" speech that still prophetically looms over our nation today.

THE INVISIBLE KINGDOM

> If Satan also be divided against himself, how shall his kingdom
> stand? because ye say that I cast out devils through Beelzebub.
> —LUKE 11:18

In verse 18 above, Jesus didn't just validate the kingdom of the devil
once; He validated it twice, in verifiable red letters. He called it
"his kingdom"—the devil's kingdom. This is a kingdom of invis-
ibility, a kingdom that wants to remain so invisible that it is never
brought to light. The sad reality is that in most churches the devil's
kingdom will never be brought to light because the leadership is
afraid to expose something they cannot see, so it remains invisible along with its wicked inner workings, never to be exposed. For
that, the kingdom of evil remains comfortable in most churches in
this nation. I never again want a church where the devil remains
comfortably invisible. There's a famous saying with an unknown
source that goes something like this: "The greatest trick the devil
ever pulled was convincing the world he doesn't exist." It's famous
because it's true. The fact that it was made famous by Hollywood
is a deep irony that will definitely preach (maybe in a future text).

There's a reason why this confrontation represents such a controversial transition in the ministry of Jesus. Did you know that
virtually every miracle you can imagine was performed in the Old
Testament except for one? In the Old Testament multitudes were
fed. Natural-disaster miracles abounded. Water came out of rocks
and bubbled up in the desert. The Red Sea was parted. People were
raised from the dead. Leprosy was cleansed. Sicknesses were cured.
Homes were reunited. Sticks turned into serpents. Water turned
into blood. The list goes on.

The Old Testament is packed full of all the miracles we see in
the New Testament except for one: a demon was never cast out of
a person before Jesus started His ministry. Why? Because people
didn't have the authority until Jesus gave it to us. As noted earlier,

we did see Saul receive temporary relief from an evil spirit when David played his harp, but without the authority of Jesus, it soon returned. This reality underscores the truth that cannot ever be diminished. Jesus is Lord of all.

THEY SHALL BE YOUR JUDGES

And if I by Beelzebub cast out devils, by whom do your sons cast them out? therefore shall they be your judges.

—LUKE 11:19

When Jesus came on the scene and did this new miracle that shocked everyone, He was already proving Himself to be the gospel personified. In verse 19 Jesus said, in effect, "Hypothetically speaking, let's just say that I really don't have the power of God and that I'm actually full of the devil Myself. Here's My question: If that were the case, then by whom do *your* sons cast demons out?"

At that time the Jews believed in a form of exorcism that did not truly bring victory because they didn't know the key element in how to get demons out: the power of Jesus' name. Jesus was basically saying, "You don't deny the reality of demonic possession, and you don't deny the reality that people are casting demons out because even your sons are doing it (though they're doing it wrong), so if you think I'm casting out devils by the power of devils—and it's working—pray tell Me, in whose name are your sons casting out devils? They will be your judges." Religious people are always guilty of hypocrisy, and even then a tree was known by its fruit, so Jesus knew this would get their attention. By this He was saying, "We will see in time who has the ministry that produces the fruit of the Spirit and who has the ministry that produces the rottenness of the flesh."

Earlier in Luke, Jesus said, "Wisdom is justified of all her children" (7:35). That verse used to make me scratch my head in bewilderment. But now I know it means that we can just let this thing play out. Time will tell. The next generation will tell you whether we were right or not. If we don't take up this mantle of deliverance and obey the Great Commission, the next generation will take it up and do it without us, and only God will know what we will have lost. In the time we've been actively engaged in deliverance ministry, I've learned that the younger generations are sick of lukewarm, watered-down, skinny-jean Christianity. They want the power of God to defeat evil; they want something that is real, and there's nothing more real than taking two kingdoms and letting them collide right before your very eyes.

THE FINGER OF GOD

> But if I with the finger of God cast out devils, no doubt the kingdom of God is come upon you.
> —LUKE 11:20

Jesus wants us to know that the casting out of evil spirits is so powerful that He equated it to the writing of the Law by the finger of God. Through this verse, Jesus said the finger of God is the power and authority by which the kingdom of God is coming to you. We all can take authority over evil spirits by the finger of God.

Textually, this is the fifth reference to the finger of God in Scripture, and it's interesting that the magicians in Egypt were among the first to reference it. They had the power to make their sticks turn into snakes, as did Moses and Aaron, but Aaron's rod swallowed theirs up. They had the power to turn water into blood and to bring up frogs and release them, but there came a moment when their magic had no power against the work of God. When Aaron and Moses lifted that rod and smote the dust of the land of Egypt, the dust turned to a plague of lice before them. In response to this relentless show of power the magicians said, "This is the finger of God," as they could not duplicate these miracles.

So, the first time the finger of God was ever recognized in the Bible, it came as a judgment upon the people of Egypt (Exod. 8:19), and the Israelites soon left Egypt after 430 years of bondage. When they crossed the parted waters of the Red Sea, the thing God used to deliver them from their enemy is the same thing God used to destroy their enemy, as the water they walked through to finally reach freedom also destroyed those who pursued them. From this we see that the God who leads you to it is the same God who will lead you through it.

In our key verse, Jesus literally recognized deliverance ministry as the finger of God. It is not the work of man's hand. It is by God's providence. The mockers and naysayers can say what they will about those of us who cast out demons in Jesus' name, but we can honestly say we have seen the finger of God work miracles over and over again! Why would we care about the criticisms of man? We're talking about the finger of God reaching down and plucking out evil spirits from people's lives, and all we have to do is obey the Great Commission to see it happen.

Notice also in our key verse that Jesus said the act of casting out devils "by the finger of God" left "no doubt the *kingdom of God* is come upon you." He later said, "The kingdom of God is within you" (Luke 17:21), and also famously said, "Thy kingdom come, Thy will be done in earth, as it is in heaven" (Matt. 6:10). And later in the Gospel of Matthew we see He also said, "Whatsoever ye shall loose on earth shall be loosed in heaven" (Matt. 18:18). All of this talk about His kingdom points to the power and authority He has given us to destroy the kingdom of evil, on earth as it is in heaven; in men today as it was in first-century Israel.

It doesn't matter what the critics and religious judges say, now or then. God has given His people authority, anointing, and equipping that we have refused for far too long. It is our fault—the church's fault—that this culture is demonized and spiraling downward. We have to repent and get right with God. We do not have a White House problem in this nation—we have a God's house problem. We need pastors to finally stand up and teach their people the whole truth of the Bible. The kingdom of God is among us through the power of the Holy Spirit whom Jesus has instructed us to ask and to put into action. If we do these things by the finger of God, then the kingdom of God has come unto us! For this we should continually ask for "more, Lord!"

> And the kingdom and dominion, and the greatness of the kingdom under the whole heaven, shall be given to the people of the saints of the most High, whose kingdom is an everlasting kingdom, and all dominions shall serve and obey him.
> —DANIEL 7:27

Chapter 7

THE WHEN AND WHERE OF JESUS

*And they went into Capernaum; and straightway on the sab-
bath day he entered into the synagogue, and taught. And
they were astonished at his doctrine: for he taught them
as one that had authority, and not as the scribes.*
—MARK 1:21–22

THE FOUR GOSPELS record thirty-seven miracles of Jesus, and
the Gospel of Mark stands out for recording the most. In
Mark chapter 1 alone we find four accounts of deliverance,
and these amazing stories all come together in a single twenty-four-
hour period in Jesus' ministry—a day in the life of Christ that gives
us an indefensible argument for why we've been preaching on the
kingdom of darkness.

Reading Mark's Gospel is like a thrill ride—everything happens
so fast. You'll notice a particular word that's used again and again:
straightway. For example, in verse 21 above we see, "And they [Jesus
and His disciples] went into Capernaum; and *straightway* on the
sabbath day he entered into the synagogue, and taught" (emphasis
added). That word *straightway* is mentioned a whopping nineteen
times in the King James Version of Mark. It means quickly or done
with expediency.

Where is Jesus going? Where He always went upon entering
a new town: the synagogue. Picture this with me. Jesus and His
disciples show up in Capernaum, and immediately Jesus makes a

beeline for the synagogue, where He opens up a scroll and starts to teach from the Word. When He does, the Scripture says "they were astonished at his doctrine" (v. 22). Notice that He has doctrine—not opinions or suggestions or commentaries. We're living in a day when people no longer take the red-letter Word of Jesus seriously. But we aim to correct that.

The word *doctrine* means teaching, so if you take doctrine out of the Bible, you take teaching out of the Bible and it becomes a free-for-all, which is exactly what we see in most churches today. The Bible is not a buffet where you get to pick and choose what you want. You have to believe and obey the whole thing, even the parts that are difficult.

So, the congregation and clergy in the synagogue were astonished at His teaching. Why? Because He "taught them as one that had authority, and not as the scribes." Right away that tells us that the scribes had no authority. They had the Law written in their scrolls. They had a bunch of rules and regulations, but they themselves had no authority. When Jesus gave us the Word with authority, He was in effect giving us the authority of His Word. When we discuss the power in "the name of Jesus," we're pointing to this authority. If the church wants to start operating in the power of this authority, we have to quit playing games and start preaching what the Bible actually says—what Jesus actually says.

TEACHING THE WORD WITH AUTHORITY CAUSES DEMONS TO MANIFEST

> And there was in their synagogue a man with an unclean spirit; and he cried out, saying, Let us alone; what have we to do with thee, thou Jesus of Nazareth? art thou come to destroy us? I know thee who thou art, the Holy One of God.
> —MARK 1:23–24

In the context of our current key passage, Jesus is in the midst of teaching, and the people are already astounded at the words coming out of His mouth, when suddenly a man with a demon begins to manifest and cries out (v. 23). It's important to realize that it wasn't the man that cried out; it was the unclean spirit inside the man. The demon inside him cried out while Jesus was preaching. Something in His preaching drew out that unclean spirit.

Now, here's what Jesus *did not* do. He did not stop and say, "Sir, you have dared to disrupt this service. I'm going to have the ushers escort you out right now so I can return to My preaching and bring peace back to the service." No. As He always did (and I'll surely remind you again), Jesus took the spirit out of the man and left the man in the synagogue, and then He used this event as a springboard to continue preaching the Word. This is how our churches must start to respond. It's what Jesus did.

DELIVERANCE INVITES CRITICISM

Notice that Jesus did not move this act of deliverance to a corner or a back room somewhere. He did it right there in the center of the synagogue. He wasn't ashamed of the power of His own name, He wasn't ashamed of the power and authority of the Word of God, and He certainly didn't shy away from the work of the Holy Spirit. He did it very publicly for all to see.

I find it especially interesting that this first recorded deliverance happened in the synagogue with a congregant. That tells us the man wasn't there to cause trouble; he was there to submit to teaching. He was sitting quietly in the service until something Jesus said stirred up the dark spirit in him, so it cried out, "Let us alone" (v. 24). From this "us" we know there was more than one dark spirit in the man. In Scripture we see that demons always come in multiples. The demon continued with, "What have we to do with thee, thou Jesus of Nazareth? art thou come to destroy us? I know thee who thou art, the Holy One of God."

It's interesting that demons will call Jesus the Son of God, and they will call Him the Holy One of God as we see here, but they will never call Him Lord. The devil won't allow it because the devil wants to be Lord. Out of a whole room full of people, including a group of disciples, it took a demon to call Jesus the Holy One of God. Nobody else acknowledged that in the service except the demons—and they were right! They knew Him then, and they know Him now.

> And Jesus rebuked him, saying, Hold thy peace, and come out of him. And when the unclean spirit had torn him, and cried with a loud voice, he came out of him. And they were all amazed, insomuch that they questioned among themselves, saying, What thing is this? what new doctrine is this? for with authority commandeth he even the unclean spirits, and they do obey him.
>
> —MARK 1:25–27

Then "Jesus rebuked him, saying, Hold thy peace, and come out of him" (v. 25). That phrase "hold thy peace" is the same phrase in the Greek that Jesus used on the deck of the ship when He said, "Peace, be still" to the wind and the waves (Mark 4:39). In hillbilly slang terminology, He said, "Shut up." After the unclean spirit had torn the man "and cried with a loud voice, he came out of him" (v. 26). Why? Because Jesus told him to.

Verse 27 tells us the people "were all amazed." You see, people still respond the same way to demons as they always have. They couldn't contain their amazement. "Did you see that? Oh my goodness, that was amazing! What new doctrine is this?"

But the truth is, this was not a new doctrine. Exorcism had been around for a long time, even before Jesus showed up, but Jesus made it successful because there was no power before He came on the scene. The doctrine of deliverance had always been there; it was the authority that was new. Jesus commanded the unclean spirits with authority, and they obeyed Him (v. 27).

> And immediately his fame spread abroad throughout all the region round about Galilee. And forthwith, when they were come out of the synagogue, they entered into the house of Simon and Andrew, with James and John. But Simon's wife's mother lay sick of a fever, and anon they tell him of her. And he came and took her by the hand, and lifted her up; and immediately the fever left her, and she ministered unto them.
>
> —MARK 1:28–31

Things begin to shift into a new context in verse 28: "And immediately his fame spread abroad throughout all the region round about Galilee." From this we know the first thing that put Jesus on the map was the act of calling out demons. Psalm 105:1 says, "O give thanks unto the LORD; call upon his name: make known his deeds among the people." God's miraculous acts have always brought fame to His name, and the Bible commands us to do the same. When we make known His deeds through preaching and practice, we bring fame to His name. It cannot be overemphasized that deliverance was the most common miraculous act of Jesus. Whenever He preached, He invariably cast out demons. Again, Scripture commands us to do the same.

As soon as Jesus and the disciples came out of the synagogue (Mark 1:29–30), they entered the house of Simon Peter and Andrew, with James and John. Simon Peter's mother-in-law lay sick with a fever, and everybody told Jesus about it. Keep in mind that Jesus had just finished casting out a devil in the synagogue. Then, in verse 31, we see that He immediately took her hand and healed her.

To fully understand what happened here, we have to read this account as recorded in the Gospel of Matthew. Talking about the same miracle, the text says Jesus came in and laid hands on her and *rebuked* the fever (Matt. 8:15). He didn't rebuke *her*. He rebuked the fever! Mark said when that transpired, Jesus lifted her up and the fever was gone. This reveals that the woman was being oppressed by a spirit of infirmity, and by rebuking it, Jesus cast it out.

It's important to know that this was the Sabbath day. By the Law of Moses, the Sabbath day had to pass and the sun had to set before any amount of work could be done. The Jews weren't even supposed to walk around or do any menial tasks on the Sabbath. Nonetheless, word traveled fast because, as the account continues in Matthew:

> That evening they brought to him many who were oppressed by demons, and he cast out the spirits with a word and healed all who were sick. This was to fulfill what was spoken by the prophet Isaiah: "He took our illnesses and bore our diseases."
> —MATTHEW 8:16–17, ESV

I'm convinced much of the physical infirmity we deal with is the result of demonic attack. Jesus rebuked the fever right after He rebuked a devil, and Peter's mother-in-law was immediately healed.

The same account, as told in parallel in Mark 1:32, says: "And at even, *when the sun did set*, they brought unto him all that were diseased, and them that were possessed with devils" (emphasis added). This is the third instance in one chapter that Jesus confronts demons who were oppressing people. He went into the synagogue and cast out a devil. He went to lunch and cast out a devil. Then folks from all over the town came to the house asking Him to cast out devils and heal the sick, so Jesus "healed many that were sick of divers diseases, and cast out many devils" (v. 34).

Early the next morning, Jesus went out and departed to a solitary place to pray. Simon Peter and a few of the other disciples followed after Him, and when they found Him they said:

> "Everyone is looking for you." And he said to them, "Let us go on to the next towns, that I may preach there also, for

that is why I came out." And he went throughout all Galilee, preaching in their synagogues and casting out demons.

—MARK 1:37–39, ESV

Read that last sentence again. Devils were cast out—again. Jesus engaged in full-on deliverance ministry on four separate occasions in one chapter. It wasn't just four individual devils; it was four different encounters with multiple devils. In fact, the third encounter involved "many" devils, and the fourth represented the largest portion of His ministry, as everywhere He went, He continued "preaching in their synagogues and casting out demons" (v. 39, ESV).

In Acts 10:38 we see this model being reinforced wherever the gospel was preached. Simon Peter was preaching to Cornelius the centurion, along with his family and friends, when he taught them "how God anointed Jesus of Nazareth with the Holy Ghost and with power: who went about doing good." Peter then goes on to tell us what constituted those "good" works: "healing all that were oppressed of the devil; for God was with him."

Through this chapter I hope it stood out to you that Jesus laid His hands upon those who were oppressed by the devil, which tells us that many if not most of the healings He performed were demon-related. As we will fully discuss later in this book, not everything that attacks us and our health is demonic, but as we learned in this chapter, we should be prepared to deal with demons whenever disease is present. And notice that Jesus was always tender with the people but forceful with the demonic influence.

As we'll find out in the next chapter, people everywhere—not just those with infirmities—are desperate for deliverance and in need of this ministry. Let's keep Jesus' approach firmly in mind as we continue to learn how to do what He did. As Peter reminded us in his first letter:

For to this you have been called, because Christ also suffered for you, leaving you an example, so that you might follow in his steps.

—1 PETER 2:21, ESV

Chapter 8

THE TORMENT OF
UNFORGIVENESS

*Judge not, and ye shall not be judged: condemn not, and ye
shall not be condemned: forgive, and ye shall be forgiven.*

—LUKE 6:37

U NFORGIVENESS IS THE biggest kink in the hose in American Christianity. It's why this nation is in such a mess right now. It's why our churches are dead and dying. It's why the lukewarm spirit of the age has destroyed our congregations. It's also the number one reason why people do not receive freedom and deliverance.

We sit in church with absolute unforgiveness in our hearts, glorying in the fact that we've been forgiven of all, yet we forgive so very little of those who have grieved us. People say, "Oh, but you don't know what they did," or, "You don't know what they said." I will never minimize what they did or said, but it pales in comparison to what we've done and what we've said to Jesus.

Ephesians 4:32 says God has forgiven us of all our sin for Jesus' sake. We deserve death, but through His forgiveness we have been given life. We deserve hell, but because of the baptism of God's love and forgiveness we've been radically set free from our rebellion and our grievances. Forgiveness is simply setting people free who don't deserve it. From a deliverance standpoint, what we most have to learn about forgiveness is that it's not about the person who wronged you being right—it's about you being right, in your spirit. In that respect, forgiveness isn't initially for the other person; it's a gift you give yourself.

HOW OFTEN, LORD?

> Then came Peter to him, and said, Lord, how oft shall my brother sin against me, and I forgive him? till seven times? Jesus saith unto him, I say not unto thee, Until seven times: but, Until seventy times seven.
>
> —MATTHEW 18:21–22

Jesus had this unique way of taking the cookies and putting them on the bottom shelf so everyone could reach them. The passage in Matthew 18 above was a very elementary teaching, yet even some of Jesus' disciples didn't quite grasp what He was saying. Here we see Simon Peter, the leader of the disciples during this time, not only asking "How often?" but also offering up his own answer. Peter had the spiritual gift of putting both feet in his mouth at the exact same time.

Peter says, "How often should I forgive the people who have ticked me off? How often should I forgive the people who have abused me? How often should I forgive the people who have hurt me?" Then Peter tries to sound super spiritual by coming up with his own super-charitable answer: "Should I forgive him a whopping *seven* times? Should I go that far above and beyond the Mosaic Law? Seven times, Lord?" Seven is the number of perfection, and you can be sure Peter knew that. Peter must have been confident that his bold answer would please his Master.

Well, Jesus fixed that quick. He said, "I say not unto thee, Until seven times: but, Until seventy times seven" (v. 22). Please do not misunderstand what Jesus meant; simple math makes that 490 times, but He was not saying to keep a record of wrongs as if you have permission to bust them in the mouth on the 491st time. Jesus was using an analogy to say we should continue to forgive an innumerable number of times because unforgiveness is a dark spirit.

This is why some of you are riddled with bitterness. It's why some of you are under a curse of turmoil financially. When you put your head on the pillow at night, all you see is the aggressor, the abuser, and the molester—the dad that walked out, the mom that ridiculed you, the fifth-grade teacher that embarrassed you, or that pastor who scarred you. In every case they were wrong, and you just can't let it go. You say things like, "If you only knew how they've ruined the last twenty years of my life." Yes, and with an attitude like that, under the torment of unforgiveness, they will ruin the next twenty years of your life as well!

For your own sake, you have to release them. You give the enemy a foothold when you are not willing to forgive people, when you refuse to forgive their wrongs against you though God has forgiven you of so much. You give the enemy a rightful place to bring in a spirit of unforgiveness. As a result, you walk around bottled up in rebellion and bitterness and can't figure out why you always snap at your spouse or get frustrated with your kids. Everybody's always on your nerves. You never have patience. You struggle with road rage. You can't even pray, and you wonder, "When will I get my break-through?" The answer is simple: when you forgive the people that hurt you and just let it go.

FORGIVEN OF ALL

Therefore is the kingdom of heaven likened unto a certain king, which would take account of his servants. And when he had begun to reckon, one was brought unto him, which owed him ten thousand talents. But forasmuch as he had not to pay, his lord commanded him to be sold, and his wife, and children, and all that he had, and payment to be made. The servant therefore fell down, and worshipped him, saying, Lord, have patience with me, and I will pay thee all. Then the lord of that servant was moved with compassion, and loosed him, and forgave him the debt.

—MATTHEW 18:23–27

Peter's question about forgiveness led Jesus to tell a parable of the kingdom. Parables are analogies with heavenly principles boiled down for us to understand with earthly recognition. In the analogy from our key passage above, Jesus tells us about a king. Though He is usually talking about God His Father when He speaks of a king in His parables, in this analogy He's referring to Himself. When the story speaks about the king's servants, He's referring to all of us.

Romans 14:12 says, "Every one of us shall give account of himself to God." The Greek word used here for *account* is *logos*, which literally means you will give a spoken account. We've all heard somebody say, "When you get to heaven, God is going to rewind the divine DVD and show you what you did with your life." But the Bible says you're actually going to open your own mouth and tell God what you did with your life.

In our key passage we get a picture of all the king's servants together in one place. They begin to count the money to figure out who has a debt, who has paid their debt off, and who owes money to whom. When the king began to reconcile the accounts, a servant who owed ten thousand talents of gold was brought before him (Matt. 18:24). Jesus uses the measure of ten thousand talents to indicate that this man owed an insurmountable debt and it wasn't likely that he could ever pay it. In fact, it was impossible for him to pay it in a thousand lifetimes—but that's the point. We must take our focus off how much the debt is worth because it doesn't really matter in the parable. A single talent of gold weighed seventy-three pounds in the Bible, and this man owed ten thousand of them. The point is that it's a debt he could not humanly pay.

The Bible never tells us how this man incurred such an unbelievable amount of debt. The assumed truth of the text is that he is simply in a mess that he cannot get out of. He could never work long enough or hard enough to pay it off. That's the point of the narrative.

Because the man could not pay, his master commanded that he be sold, along with his wife, his children, and all that he had, to make payment toward the debt (Matt. 18:25). Take notice of the fact that his poor decision did not just affect him; it affected his whole family and his household. We all need to realize that our poor decisions will affect everybody around us. No man lives unto himself, and no man dies unto himself. We affect people, good or bad, with every decision we make.

So, the king simply said, "I'm going to put you in jail. Everybody's going to be sold, and payment will be made. You're all going to work this off in blood, sweat, and tears every day of your lives until the debt is paid." As king, he had the prerogative to do that. We might think the king is a bully, but be reminded that he did nothing wrong in the context of the parable.

Then things change drastically in verse 26 as the servant falls down, groveling in repentance. He knew he was in the wrong, so he fell down and worshipped the king, pleading for debt relief and forgiveness: "Lord, have patience with me and I will pay thee all." It was a statement of desperation. He knew he was going to prison and his family would be sold into servitude. Even if he was given one thousand years, it would never be enough time. Jesus ensured we understood the gravity of the teaching.

MOVED WITH COMPASSION

In verse 27 we see that the lord in the parable was moved with compassion. He wasn't arrogant. He didn't demand that the law be upheld, and he didn't call his lawyers. He was deeply moved because the man fell down in true repentance and humility, pleading, "Please don't sell my wife. Please don't take my kids. Please don't take away my home and all my land. If you just give me more time, I'll pay all I owe you, Lord." That's when the one with the authority—the king—rose up to change the situation. Only the king could make the situation worse or relieve the man of the debt and make the situation better.

The king chose the latter and forgave the man of his debt (v. 27). Now, before we go any further, we must understand what Jesus is trying to propagate in our hearts. The king, knowing the man could not pay him, and seeing his submission and humility, said, "I'm going to do better than give you more time. I'm going to relinquish the debt. I'm going to absolve you of every single financial obligation you have to me. I'm going to forgive it all." Get that picture in your mind. The man owed a debt he could never repay, and the king erased all of it simply because he was a man of compassion and forgiveness.

This is a glorious picture of the gospel of Jesus Christ. You owed a debt to God you could never pay back. It was spiritually impossible for you to purchase your own forgiveness, and yet He gave it freely. Seeing the servant's humility and repentance, the king stood up on his throne of glory and said, "Through your repentance, I'm moved with compassion. I forgive you of all your sin. I forgive you of all your rebellion. I forgive all of it." In response to our humility and repentance, God forgave us a debt we could never pay back. We were dead in our sins and hell-bound, but the grace of God forgave us of everything. The Bible says "if we confess our sins, he is faithful and just to forgive us our sins, and to cleanse us from all unrighteousness" (1 John 1:9).

Every sin you've ever committed or ever will commit has been washed away in the forgiving blood of Calvary. He's forgiven us all of our debt. We don't have to go to bed tonight wondering which sins He's forgiven and which ones He's overlooked and forgotten to forgive. Jesus canceled our debt—not just some of it; He canceled every drop of it. He knew that our rebellion had gotten us into a jam. We could try to beg our way out in futility or borrow our way out and just get deeper into debt, but He made a way where there seemed to be no way. That's why the Bible says, "Not by works of righteousness which we have done, but according to his mercy he saved us, by the washing of regeneration, and renewing of the Holy Ghost" (Titus 3:5). And this: "For by grace are ye saved through faith; and that not of yourselves: it is the gift of God: not of works, lest any man should boast" (Eph. 2:8–9).

We have nothing to boast about other than Jesus. He's the King who forgave the debt you and I owed!

As we continue in Matthew 18, we see the parable take a disturbing turn.

FORGIVEN BUT NOT FORGIVING?

> But the same servant went out, and found one of his fellowservants, which owed him an hundred pence: and he laid hands on him, and took him by the throat, saying, Pay me that thou owest. And his fellowservant fell down at his feet, and besought him, saying, Have patience with me, and I will pay thee all. And he would not: but went and cast him into prison, till he should pay the debt.
>
> —MATTHEW 18:28–30

Here is where things get interesting. At the time when Jesus told this story a hundred pence was like a day's wages. So, for the sake of illustration, let's say the man owed the king $10 million and was forgiven of every cent, including the interest, and now the man has found someone who owes him $100.

So the man (the first servant) grabs ahold of the second servant, snatches him by the throat, and demands repayment. He immediately takes his impatience and frustration out on this man. And we all say, "Wait a minute; this is the same guy that was just forgiven so much?" Yep. This is the same man who had just been forgiven the greatest debt imaginable. This is the only parable Jesus ever told with such financial magnitude, as it was intended to stand out. God was showing us just how much the blood of Jesus has forgiven us. In the parable, the first servant refused to give the same grace on a far smaller level that he'd just received at such a magnanimous level. He refused to show even an ounce of compassion.

We can read this and easily think Jesus was talking about the single man's stupidity, but He's talking about the stupidity of everyone, including you and me. We've all been forgiven of it all and yet can't forgive that one person. We can't let that one person go who ticked us off, that one person who hurt us, walked away from us, abandoned us, or embarrassed us.

Now, we're never told to celebrate the hurt they brought. The enemy used these offenders to open a door that has caused dark spirits to follow us and oppress us our entire lives. The only way to break that cycle is to forgive the people we don't want to forgive. No matter what they said or did, in comparison to what Jesus has forgiven us, it's small change. It's $100 in comparison to $10 million. Who do we think we're really hurting?

We're holding these people hostage in our hearts, saying, "I'm not answering her phone call...I'm not even going to look at them...I can't even go to the same church." We have been relieved of our own sinful wickedness before God and yet we are not willing to relieve one or two or ten people who have hurt us. We still can't even pray without their faces popping up in our minds. This is why some of us will never go to the next level in our deliverance. Forgiveness is the gift we give ourselves, and we have to give it to receive it (Luke 6:37). We have to forgive others to cast out the spirit of unforgiveness.

People cause such division in the body of Christ, and God absolutely hates it. The Book of Proverbs lists this as one of the top seven things God hates: a proud look, hands that shed innocent blood, and sowing discord among the brethren (Prov. 6:16–19). People sow discord because they have unforgiveness in their hearts. They're miserable, so they want everybody else to be miserable. They want other people to feel the torment they feel. They have people by the throat who owe them little to nothing, and they won't forgive despite having been forgiven so much more. Isn't it easy to see a dark spirit at work in this pattern? As we continue with the parable, we see this pattern emerge.

> And his fellowservant fell down at his feet, and besought him, saying, Have patience with me, and I will pay thee all. And he would not: but went and cast him into prison, till he should pay the debt. So when his fellowservants saw what was done, they were very sorry, and came and told unto their lord all that was done. Then his lord, after that he had called him, said unto him, O thou wicked servant, I forgave thee all that debt, because thou desiredst me: Shouldest not thou also have had compassion on thy fellowservant, even as I had pity on thee?
>
> —MATTHEW 18:29–33

In verse 29 we see the first servant grab his fellow servant by the throat. Imagine his debtor slipping out of his hands and falling to the ground, pleading, "Have patience with me, and I will pay thee all." Notice that's the exact phrase the first servant used on his lord when he was forgiven. Jesus then tells us that the first servant put his fellow servant in jail until the whole debt was paid.

Once the king was alerted to this sad turn, he called the man before him again. Notice the king still called him a servant. He didn't say, "You wicked person." He said, "You wicked servant." Remember that this is a parable of the kingdom, and we are all represented by this servant. God didn't have to save us. God could let every one of us burn in hell and He would still be God, but He didn't. He had pity because we asked Him to forgive us. We called unto Him, and He heard and answered us. He showed us great and mighty things—and forgiveness—which we know not without Him. Shouldn't we have pity on others as God has had compassion on us? Shouldn't we do for others what Jesus did for us?

God's Response to Unforgiveness

When we live in unforgiveness, we make very unwise choices. We hurt people. We rebel against the things of God while thinking we're being spiritual. We try to justify unforgiveness by finding out-of-context Bible verses to make us feel better about not doing what God clearly called us to do, refusing to do for others what Jesus clearly did for us. All the while, we're trying to find human methods to make ourselves sleep better at night, but the problem is that we're in torment. As we reach the conclusion of the parable, we see this behavior has devastating consequences.

> And his lord was wroth, and delivered him to the tormentors, till he should pay all that was due unto him. So likewise shall my heavenly Father do also unto you, if ye from your hearts forgive not every one his brother their trespasses.
> —MATTHEW 18:34–35

The same king who forgave the man of all his debts was greatly angered and said, in effect, "I'm going to let the tormentors take care of you. I'm going to let them deal with you till you pay all that was due unto me, which would have been nothing had you forgiven, but now it will be impossible." By this the parable tells us this man's torment will be endless. But then watch what Jesus says in verse 35: "So likewise shall my heavenly Father do also unto you." Did Jesus really just say that in red letters? Yes, He said the Father will deliver you to the tormentors. We've come to understand that the tormentors are the spirit of unforgiveness, the spirit of bitterness, and the spirit of offense, among others. Just as an evil spirit came upon Saul in the Old Testament, you will be tormented by evil spirits that God will allow until you break the cycle and truly forgive.

You may say, "Well, I just can't bring myself to forgiveness, and I just can't let it go." You'd be in hell if God thought that way. He's forgiven you the full debt. Please understand that your forgiveness doesn't minimize the pain and abuse these people put you through, but you have to trust God to sort all of that out. If you are waiting for them to repent, just let it go. God will deal with them. His justice is inescapable. You simply cannot allow everyone else in your life to suffer from the work of the tormentors in you just because you can't forgive others.

From this parable you know that when you refuse to forgive, you give place to evil spirits that aim to destroy you. You literally give demons the legal right before God to invade you (v. 35), and the person who hurt you won't feel a thing. Until you forgive, the spirit of unforgiveness can and will bring all its friends into your life like a gang of cowards: *shame* that's not yours to bear, *guilt* that has never been yours to carry, and *anger* and *impatience* that will torment you. Bitterness will eventually consume you. It's all clear to see in light of this parable.

We have to supernaturally forgive the people in our lives that we naturally don't want to. We have to let them go. Otherwise, there is no use for us to talk about our deliverance because the deliverance we need is deliverance from ourselves—from our unforgiveness. The Lord's Prayer even says, "Forgive us our trespasses, as we forgive those who trespass against us." (See Matthew 6:9–13.) That's not easy to do, but if we want to be delivered, we have no other choice. We have to forgive that offender and quit letting them live rent-free in our heads.

When I went through deliverance, I didn't just have to forgive a couple of people. I had to forgive a whole denomination. I had to forgive pastors who hurt me, ministries I worked for, and a college that abandoned me. I had some deep levels of unforgiveness to deal with.

The interesting thing about unforgiveness is that looking back, you recognize that a lot of your foolish decisions were made while holding people by the throat. You punished them out of a spirit of unforgiveness toward someone else. Some of you have been given over to the tormentor, and it shows.

At the end of the parable Jesus says nothing about the second servant being tormented, though he may indeed have harmed the first. Instead, the story tragically ends with the first servant being choked and tormented in a prison he created with his unforgiveness.

Are you ready to be delivered from this dark spirit? Declare today as a day of freedom and march around your Jericho, shouting that the walls of unforgiveness must fall down in your life. Break that legal contract today by forgiving all and letting them go, and deliverance will follow. Now that you know the truth about unforgiveness, you're accountable to it, because to whom much is given, much shall be required (Luke 12:48), so please don't ignore this red-letter message.

May God allow all torment through unforgiveness to fall to the ground like broken chains and free us of the prisons of our own making. Beloved, let's learn this principle of the kingdom and freely forgive others as we have been so freely forgiven.

> And as ye go, preach, saying, The kingdom of heaven is at hand. Heal the sick, cleanse the lepers, raise the dead, cast out devils: freely ye have received, freely give.
> —MATTHEW 10:7–8

Chapter 9

WE WALK AS JESUS WALKED

And when the devil had ended all the temptation, he
departed from him for a season. And Jesus returned in
the power of the Spirit into Galilee: and there went out
a fame of him through all the region round about. And
he taught in their synagogues, being glorified of all.

—LUKE 4:13–15

WHEN THE DEVIL tempted Jesus in the wilderness, Jesus responded the same way every time—and through His example He showed us how to resist the devil (Jas. 4:7). What He *did not* do was carry on a psychological evaluation of the devil. He *did not* come to him with all types of educated jargon. And He *did not* waste His time arguing or debating with him. Jesus simply said, "It is written…it is written…it is written…" There is still power in the Word of the living God. The anointing is upon the Word, and if you stay in the Word, the anointing will be upon you. As I discussed in great detail in *Weapons of Our Warfare*, the Word of God is the two-edged *sword of the Spirit*—the most powerful weapon in the armor of God. The devil simply can't stand up to the Word because it exposes him for who he is.

As noted earlier, deliverance is not a methodology, so though I'll discuss how Jesus and the disciples and other believers battled devils as chronicled throughout the New Testament, I'm not going to be giving you a formula beyond that which the Holy Spirit gives us through the Bible. It all starts and ends with His sword—the Word of God. Know the Word, speak the Word, and take authority in Jesus' name as taught in the Word, and the Holy Spirit will do the rest. If you are a born-again believer, you can and will do what Jesus did once you know His ways as detailed in His Word. When Jesus battled Satan in the wilderness, He didn't battle in the flesh but in the spirit, and all He needed was the piercing power of the Word of God. So, when you speak the Word in His name—in His authority—you can expect the same results (Mark 16:17).

At the end of the forty days in the wilderness, after Jesus repelled the devil with the Word of God after each temptation, the Gospel of Luke tells us that Jesus "returned in the power of the Spirit into Galilee" (4:14). This passage illustrates an undeniable principle: you will never receive more power from God until you endure testing, but once you endure, greater power *will* come. The apostle Paul said, "Most gladly therefore will I rather glory in my infirmities, that the power of Christ may rest upon me" (2 Cor. 12:9).

For this we know there are no shortcuts to spiritual power. Jesus came back from His test in the wilderness with greater power, and everybody knew it. If you want to get hooked into that power, stop trying to run or evacuate every time God allows problems to come into your life because those problems can mold and prepare you for the power.

Luke goes on to tell us, "And there went out a fame of him through all the region round about. And he taught in their synagogues, being glorified of all" (vv. 14–15). As we discussed earlier, the Gospel of Mark tells us that Jesus cast out demons most everywhere He preached, and this one-two punch of teaching the good news and casting out unclean spirits brought Him instant fame throughout all Galilee (Mark 1:27–28). Likewise, wherever Jesus went, nine times out of ten He taught in such a way that the common people received it with joy and the religious people got mad. The same was true when He cast out demons—the common folks were amazed, and the Pharisees were enraged. That's still true today.

JESUS DECLARES WHY HE CAME

> And he came to Nazareth, where he had been brought up: and, as his custom was, he went into the synagogue on the sabbath day, and stood up for to read. And there was delivered unto him the book of the prophet Esaias. And when he had opened the book, he found the place where it was written...
>
> —LUKE 4:16–17

As we continue our look into Luke 4 with verse 16, we find Jesus, fresh from His temptation in the wilderness, in the synagogue in His hometown where He grew up. When He stands up to read the Scripture to the people, He is handed the Book of Isaiah, and He is about to rock their world with the Word of God. When He opens the scroll, He finds "the place where it was written," as He knows exactly what He is there to say (Luke 4:17). In modern Bibles we can find this passage by turning to Isaiah 61.

This chapter is especially meaningful to me, as Isaiah 61:1 has always been my life verse. I chose it as a sixteen-year-old, while I was still ignorant of the Bible, because it was the verse the Holy Ghost used to call me to preach. I had no idea it was the prophetic life verse of all that Jesus did and all that Jesus was, as we see here in Luke. I later found it interesting to learn it was also the life verse of the late, great Billy Sunday, whom I wrote about earlier in this book series. When I chose it, I had no idea the verse would so radically influence me, or that years later it would inspire me to start Global Vision and engrave it on our pulpit.

Over the years, I thought I understood the contextual flow of Isaiah 61:1, but I never truly received the full revelation of what it meant until I took a deep dive into Luke 4:18–19 with renewed eyes many years later. When Jesus read this verse, He was declaring the prophetic fulfillment of the flow of His ministry as written by

Isaiah centuries earlier, with all the friends of His youth in attendance. Watch what happens:

> The Spirit of the Lord is upon me, because he hath anointed
> me to preach the gospel to the poor; he hath sent me to heal
> the brokenhearted, to preach deliverance to the captives, and
> recovering of sight to the blind, to set at liberty them that are
> bruised, to preach the acceptable year of the Lord.
> —JESUS (LUKE 4:18–19)

I have quoted this passage probably ten thousand times through the years, but not the Luke 4:18–19 version. When I read the Luke version shortly after removing my denominational lens, it enveloped my heart in a whole new, prophetic way. I began to understand what Jesus really meant when He said in Luke 19:10, "[I came] to seek and to save that which was lost." He did not just come to be a handyman. He did not just come to do miracles, though the miracles validated the message He preached. He came to save the world (John 12:47).

In 2 Corinthians 5:21 we read, "For he hath made him to be sin for us, who knew no sin; that we might be made the righteousness of God in him." Jesus is the gospel. But in the context of our passage in Luke, His hometown crowd wasn't impressed. As we learn from the Gospel of John, "His own received him not" (John 1:11).

Notice the progression of this reading from Luke 4, starting at verse 18: "The Spirit of the Lord is upon me because he hath anointed me to preach the gospel to the poor." In saying this, Jesus is not just talking about people who are impoverished. He's referring to the fact that every person born of a woman is born in a poor spiritual condition.

We were all born into original sin, "as by one man sin entered into the world, and death by sin; and so death passed upon all men, for that all have sinned" (Rom. 5:12). Even the richest person on the planet is bankrupt without Jesus.

THE PROGRESSION OF JESUS' MINISTRY

As we continue with Jesus' reading in Luke chapter 4, we then see "he hath sent me to heal the brokenhearted" (v. 18). Once God opened my eyes and heart to the prophetic nature of Luke 4:17–19 in my own life, I saw something I'd never paid attention to before: there is a natural progression in the ministry of Jesus. Note that the gospel always comes first. Nothing else we do even matters without the truth of the gospel. Jesus is saying, in effect, "What you do first is preach the gospel, and then the results of the gospel—the tangible results; the miracles, signs, and wonders—will follow." Also in the progression we see He goes from saving us from our sin to the mercy, grace, love, compassion, and forgiveness of God that heals our broken hearts emotionally.

There is a balm in Gilead; there is an ointment in the Savior, the Lord Jesus Christ, by which your broken heart can be mended, healed, and restored. So the progression that Jesus has outlined for His ministry is 1) saving us through the gospel, and then 2) beginning the miraculous work of inner healing. Jesus is telling us He is going to connect us emotionally to our Creator and get us past all the things that caused us to be brokenhearted to begin with.

The progression continues with 3) preaching deliverance to the captives. From this we know people are captive. They're in bondage. They're in chains and need to be delivered in Jesus' name. This, of course, is why Jesus sought to cast out demons everywhere He went.

The next thing Jesus does in this progression is 4) healing our infirmities. From this we learn that everyone who needs healing should first be delivered, as deliverance can clearly lead to miraculous healings.

As we discussed earlier, Acts 10:38 tells us that Jesus went about doing good, filled with the anointing of the Holy Ghost, healing everyone oppressed of the devil. This tells us there is a direct link between deliverance and healing. It also reveals that when Jesus laid hands on people who had infirmities, these infirmities often stemmed from demonic oppression. Throughout the gospel record, including the Great Commission in Mark 16, we see this was the way of Jesus. In the Gospel of Matthew we see "they brought to him many who were oppressed by demons, and he cast out the spirits with a word and healed all who were sick" (8:16, ESV). When Jesus called His twelve disciples, He "gave them authority over unclean spirits, to cast them out, and to heal every disease and every affliction" (10:1, ESV). When Jesus healed people, He first cast out evil spirits, and then came the healing.

I've learned that you will never get complete healing if you are still dealing with an evil spirit. You first have to be delivered from the spirit so the healing can come.

Through this progression Jesus is teaching us to minister as He ministered, to walk as He walked (1 John 2:5–6):

- We preach the gospel.

- We heal people inwardly and emotionally.

- We preach deliverance and set them free.

- We heal them in Jesus' name.

For a final word from Isaiah 61, in verse 3 we see that God offers "the garment of praise for the spirit of heaviness." I want to ensure you realize the infirmity the medical community calls *depression*, God calls the *spirit of heaviness*. If you have the spirit of heaviness and believe the authority of the Word of God, you can cast out depression and tear down the strongholds that may remain, and it will no longer be in your life. We'll discuss strongholds later in this book.

To close our study of our key passage from Luke 4, notice that Jesus closes His reading by noting the final facet of His progression, "to preach the acceptable year of the Lord" (4:19). Then He closes the book, gives it to the minister, and sits down with the eyes of all who are in the synagogue "fastened on him" (v. 20). From a seated position in a packed-out religious auditorium, with everyone looking at Him, Jesus then says, "This day is this scripture fulfilled in your ears" (v. 21). Jesus is saying, in effect, "Look, this is *Me*—I'm *Lord*, and this is the year! This is that time! It all starts now!"

The people became enraged. They all got stirred up with violent intent. They immediately wanted to kill Jesus, and so they tried. It indeed had begun. Truly, a prophet is never accepted in his own country (v. 24), let alone the Lord Himself. Jesus was willing to preach the truth at the expense of everyone hating Him for it—even unto death—and the truth is that He came to set the captives free!

> Whoever says "I know him" but does not keep his commandments is a liar, and the truth is not in him, but whoever keeps his word, in him truly the love of God is perfected. By this we may know that we are in him: whoever says he abides in him ought to walk in the same way in which he walked.
>
> —1 JOHN 2:4–6, ESV

Chapter 10

THE DEEPEST MYSTERIES
OF DELIVERANCE

Then was brought unto him one possessed with a devil,
blind, and dumb: and he healed him, insomuch that the
blind and dumb both spake and saw. And all the people
were amazed, and said, Is not this the son of David? But
when the Pharisees heard it, they said, This fellow doth not
cast out devils, but by Beelzebub the prince of the devils.
—JESUS (MATTHEW 12:22–24)

Y OU'LL PROBABLY RECOGNIZE the historic confrontation above
from our discussion in chapter 6, where we looked at it as
recorded in the Gospel of Luke. While I continue to explore
the authority and power Jesus gave us over unclean spirits, in this
chapter I want to solve two very controversial deliverance teachings
that are found in this same discourse as recorded in the Gospel of
Matthew. Chapter 12 of this Gospel is especially rich—and controversial. It's literally packed with familiar red-letter verses from the
lips of the Savior, but too many armchair theologians have chopped
up the central discourse into slices that tickle ears but ignore the
full context of Jesus' complex series of teachings.

Likewise, the widespread ignorance (and rejection) of the present
power of the Holy Spirit and His miracle of deliverance has blocked
many good Christians from seeing these deeper truths. I was formerly in that number, so I hope this chapter goes a long way to

setting them free. The first mystery we're going to unfold deals directly with the judgment that is soon to come—in the most eternally foreboding terms possible—so let's dive right in.

As we see in our key passage above, Jesus had just cast out a demon when the Pharisees accused Him of delivering the man by way of demonic power. In His profoundly rich and sobering response, Jesus brought to light what we call the *unpardonable sin*:

> Wherefore I say unto you, All manner of sin and blasphemy shall be forgiven unto men: but the blasphemy against the Holy Ghost shall not be forgiven unto men. And whosoever speaketh a word against the Son of man, it shall be forgiven him: but whosoever speaketh against the Holy Ghost, it shall not be forgiven him, neither in this world, neither in the world to come.
>
> —JESUS (MATTHEW 12:31–32)

BLASPHEMY OF THE HOLY SPIRIT

When discussing the blasphemy of the Holy Spirit, it's crucial to understand the full context of this discourse. When Jesus referred to this particular category of blasphemy as the unpardonable sin, He emphasized that while it is possible to blaspheme Him, God the Son—*the Son of man*—and still find forgiveness, a person cannot blaspheme God the Holy Spirit and expect to receive forgiveness in this life or the life to come.

Sin doesn't get any more serious than that. There has been much conjecture over the centuries concerning what exactly blaspheming the Holy Spirit is, and the theological misinterpretations are all over the map even to this day. But once you take an honest reading of this confrontation in its full context (Matt. 12:22–37), the answer is undeniable. Blaspheming the Holy Spirit is when you see a miraculous work of the Holy Spirit operating through someone but you say the source is an evil spirit. In making such a blasphemous claim, you would be saying that the Holy Spirit is an unclean spirit—a demonic power. I'm a firm believer that we should always let the Bible explain the Bible, and when we review the parallel teaching as recorded in chapter 3 of the Gospel of Mark, also in the context of Jesus casting out demons, we see blasphemy of the Holy Spirit clearly defined when Jesus said this to the Pharisees:

> Verily I say unto you, All sins shall be forgiven unto the sons of men, and blasphemies wherewith soever they shall blaspheme: But he that shall blaspheme against the Holy Ghost hath never forgiveness, but is in danger of eternal damnation. Because they said, He hath an unclean spirit.
>
> —MARK 3:28–30

Why did Jesus warn the Pharisees of the "eternal damnation" that results from blaspheming the Holy Spirit? Because they claimed the Spirit operating in Jesus—the Holy Spirit of God—was "an unclean spirit." That's blasphemy of the highest order. In our key passage from Matthew 12, Jesus plainly states that the Holy Spirit will not forgive you for speaking such blasphemy against Him.

That's a short way to say you'd better be careful that you don't try to destroy, discredit, or demonize the work of God—making yourself look and sound spiritual in the process—just because you don't believe or understand what is happening. So if you see the power of the Holy Spirit on display in this world, do not puff yourself up and make the mistake of saying it is the work of devils. That probably won't age well.

As was often the case throughout the New Testament, the Pharisees in this confrontation were operating under the spirit of religion, which is demonic, and it showed.

> But if you have bitter jealousy and selfish ambition in your hearts, do not boast and be false to the truth. This is not the

wisdom that comes down from above, but is earthly, unspiritual, demonic.

—JAMES 3:14–15, ESV

LACK OF UNDERSTANDING

As we continue in Matthew 12, still in the context of this blasphemy and the poor judgment that can cause it, Jesus continued by saying that when the end comes, God will judge the good from the evil by their fruit (v. 33), and that evil people speak evil out of the abundance of their hearts (vv. 34–35). Jesus then said that the evil will be judged harshly for every idle word they speak (v. 36), "For by thy words thou shalt be justified, and by thy words thou shalt be condemned" (v. 37). So, we know that men will be judged harshly—possibly even be *condemned*—for the evil they speak, even when it's simply "idle" conjecture. Blasphemy of the Holy Spirit is clearly a spoken offense that brings such condemnation. If you're new to the supernatural workings of God, when something happens that you don't understand, be careful to check your tongue (Jas. 3).

Aside from their blasphemy, in more rational terms the Pharisees were basically telling Jesus, "We don't understand Your methodology. Therefore, You must be wrong." We in the church have judged too many people by their methodology rather than their message. Sometimes people's methodology differs. This was a tough pill for me to swallow during my transition out of the dead religion of my past, and it produced a huge hurdle during my transition into operating in the gifts. Another preacher's methods are not my methods. My methods are not their methods. Too many people get belligerent and start disqualifying and discrediting what they see or hear in other ministries just because it doesn't line up with how God speaks to them or how God operates through them.

In this discourse Jesus was directing His words to the Pharisees—the religious crowd. In addition to warning them not to blaspheme the Holy Spirit, He was also cautioning them to measure all their words wisely and not to dismiss something or someone as false just because they didn't understand them.

We have to realize that we can never judge whether someone is real or false by how loud or quiet they are, by the denominational tag they wear, by how well they sing songs, by the color of their skin, or by anything else about their appearance. You can tell whether someone is real or false only by looking at their fruit. The fruit is the fundamental measure of whether they are true or not.

For a biblical example, let's look at the prophet Elijah. The Bible says God spoke to Elijah in a still, small voice.

> And he said, Go forth, and stand upon the mount before the LORD. And, behold, the LORD passed by, and a great and strong wind rent the mountains, and brake in pieces the rocks before the LORD; but the LORD was not in the wind; and after the wind an earthquake; but the LORD was not in the earthquake: and after the earthquake a fire; but the LORD was not in the fire: and after the fire a still small voice.
>
> —1 KINGS 19:11–12

Just because the Bible says that God was not in the fire, the whirlwind, or the earthquake when He spoke to Elijah, it doesn't mean God never speaks in these ways. It simply means in Elijah's life, that's not how God spoke or revealed Himself. What if Elijah had said, "God only speaks in a still, small voice. He *never* speaks in the fire. He *never* speaks during the earthquake. And He *never* speaks in the whirlwind." Do you know what he would have done? He would have thrown Job under the bus because God did not speak to Job in a still, small voice. God spoke to Job out of a whirlwind. God can reveal Himself to the church however He wants. He's God.

THE RETURNING DEMONS PRINCIPLE

> When the unclean spirit is gone out of a man, he walketh through dry places, seeking rest, and findeth none. Then he

saith, I will return into my house from whence I came out; and when he is come, he findeth it empty, swept, and garnished. Then goeth he, and taketh with himself seven other spirits more wicked than himself, and they enter in and dwell there: and the last state of that man is worse than the first. Even so shall it be also unto this wicked generation.

—JESUS (MATTHEW 12:43–45)

As we continue in Matthew 12, I aim to address and dispel what I consider a theological wives' tale—a deliverance fable that has scared many people away from deliverance ministry. In doing so, we're going to discuss a principle that should inspire you. At Global Vision we got baptized into deliverance ministry with such urgency that we often had to step out in faith in an effort to set them free. The people were desperate for healing and deliverance, and many were in torment, so we answered the call with all we had in us.

When you get heavily involved in a deliverance ministry like ours, people in great need frequently seek your help. We don't bemoan it; we thank God for it. So when people literally lined up down the street for ministry, we quickly transitioned into mass deliverance services to meet their needs as quickly as possible. Through the process, we eventually discovered that for many people, a subtle misunderstanding of a single phrase in Matthew 12 was blocking the door.

Early on, folks began to express concerns about undergoing deliverance due to the incomplete interpretation of Matthew 12:43–45. I frequently heard people say, "I don't want to go through deliverance because the Bible says that once you do, the demons might come back seven times worse. Why would I want to subject myself to that?" I hadn't yet received the full revelation of the principle we're about to discuss, so I understood their concerns and even reinforced them, but I also began searching for the solution in the Bible. Praise God, we can now fully dispel those concerns.

The principle of a demon returning to the house from which it left has been misused with "spooktacular" effect in deliverance ministry in a way that I'm convinced has kept more people in bondage than it has set free. In deliverance, we first must determine whether the people are saved or lost. We don't make a habit of casting demons out of lost people because the demons will easily come back. If a person is not saved through repentance and faith in the gospel, submitting their lives to the lordship of Jesus Christ, they indeed remain vulnerable to their demons. The only way to effectively cast demons out of a lost person is to first get them saved and then deal with them from a deliverance standpoint.

However, this principle isn't about whether Christians or non-Christians can have demons or whether to call it oppression, possession, or any other label. It's about how we've missed the meaning of Jesus' words in a single phrase. Upon closer examination, you will discover that Jesus was not talking about someone who experienced some improper or flawed type of deliverance resulting in the demon returning with seven others. Jesus was passionately discussing the situation of a person who has never gone through deliverance at all. In such cases, the enemy can indeed return at will because the demon was never properly expelled, so the door was never closed.

Matthew 12:43 says, "When the unclean spirit is *gone out* of a man..." (emphasis added). Here we see Jesus use a very interesting phrase that could explain why we've missed this for so long. If you ever needed proof that every single word in the Bible matters, here you go. In this phrase, Jesus uses different words for this demonic movement than what we read in Mark 6:7–13. In this passage, Jesus gave His disciples the power to expel demons, and when they went out they did exactly that: "And he called unto him the twelve, and began to send them forth two by two; and gave them power over unclean spirits" (v. 7). "And they *cast out* many devils, and anointed with oil many that were sick, and healed them" (v. 13, emphasis added).

So we see the term *cast out* (expel) used when someone is delivered in Jesus' name. But in Matthew 12, the phrase *gone out* does not come from the word for *expel*; it is from the word for *exit*. This new principle does not apply to a demon *driven out* of someone through deliverance. It refers to a demon *choosing to leave by its own will.*

There are a few things you need to know about demons. First, demons have a will. That's what damned them to hell to begin with. Second, demons can only be in one place at one time, but they can be anywhere they want at any given time.

There are times when a demon chooses, of its own volition, to exit a person and it's not because anyone drove him out, prophesied him out, or screamed him out. From our key passage in Matthew 12 we learn that when an unclean spirit has chosen to leave someone, for whatever reason, he roams around looking for another host. He's looking for somebody else to enter. He's looking for another doorway, another portal, another gateway, another highway. Maybe he's bored with a single home, and maybe he's seeking greater peace. Whatever his motivations, we know that eventually he'll start seeking *rest*. Of course, he doesn't get any rest because he knows what's coming soon.

As we see in one of Jesus' earlier encounters where the demons cried, "Have you come here to torment us before the time?" the demons know they are going to hell (Matt. 8:29, ESV). So the demon in our key passage is seeking some sort of respite, knowing that the great and dreadful day of the Lord is coming soon.

Then, in Matthew 12:44, the demon says, "I will return." So we know he had the ability to walk out by his own will, and now we see he had the same ability to turn around and walk back in. Don't miss this. While it's common for deliverance ministers to say a demon that was cast out of a person will return, we can't find anywhere in the Bible that says a demon that was cast out ever returned to the host. In fact, in Mark 9:25, when Jesus cast a demon out of a deaf and dumb boy, we see:

> And when Jesus saw that a crowd came running together, he rebuked the unclean spirit, saying to it, "You mute and deaf spirit, I command you, come out of him and never enter him again."
>
> —MARK 9:25, ESV

Jesus never once gave us an example of a demon coming back after being driven out, but here He gave us a perfect example of how to close the door. Jesus told the demon, in effect, "You can't come back no matter how much you want to."

The truth is clear: Either we have authority over serpents and scorpions (Luke 10:19) or we don't. Either it is within our power to command them to leave in Jesus' name or it is not. Jesus, as our example, demonstrated that not only can we expel these spiritual forces, but we also have the ability to permanently *evict* them from people's lives.

EXIT VS. EXPEL

So, can a demon come back? Yes, it is still a possibility, but not nearly as much a possibility as most of us thought. Some deliverance ministers have spooked people into believing an unbiblical principle, so we need to correct that immediately. We need to realize that the person mentioned in Matthew 12:43–45 was not someone from whom a demon had been cast out; it was someone from whom a demon had voluntarily departed.

When someone goes through deliverance, their body is no longer the home of a demon. But when someone hasn't gone through deliverance, their demons can come in and out whenever they choose. They simply exited the house of their own free will, so there is nothing to stop them from returning. They haven't been expelled or evicted. They go to and fro and come back as they wish, and when they do return—as Jesus tells us—it's only going to get worse for the host (Matt. 12:45).

The demon basically says to himself, "I'm going back to my old house. I'm going back to my familiar host. I wasn't driven out, I wasn't evicted, and I certainly wasn't told that I couldn't come back. I have the volition to leave and the volition to return. I have legal rights that were never revoked. I will return unto my house *from whence I came out*."

When Jesus gave us authority over demons, it was intended to drive out, cast out, take out, and evict them with full legal rights. Do you know what happens when somebody gets evicted? They don't get to say, "Wait a minute, that's my legal home, and that's all my stuff in there!" No. To that we simply say, "In Jesus' name, you got kicked out, Jack. It's not your house anymore. And if you don't drag your stuff out with you, you'll lose it because the contract says it's no longer yours. You've been evicted!"

But the demon from our key passage was not evicted. He was only in exit mode. He said, "I'm going back to my house. It's my body. It's my cottage. It's my cabin. It's my mansion. It's my place. It's my primary abode. Nobody made me leave; I just felt like leaving. But now I'm bored and restless, so I'm going back."

Once the demon has returned, "he findeth it empty, swept, and garnished" (Matt. 12:44). Do you know what I've seen nearly every day as a pastor and deliverance minister? People tormented by dreams, nightmares, addiction, heaviness, fear, anxiety, and PTSD. Do you know what happens when a demon just decides to up and leave that person for a while? The person's life suddenly goes back to a relatively normal state because they are empty of the demon—for now.

We see it all the time, among both lost people and saved people. To illustrate this new principle, consider the following allegory.

THE ALLEGORY OF THE EMPTY HOUSE

Imagine a wife who, seemingly out of nowhere, experiences a spirit of heaviness. She feels so heavily burdened that she's unable to get out of bed. She soon becomes consumed by sorrow, hurt, and a relentless spirit of offense. You ask her what is wrong, and she struggles to articulate what's troubling her. Gradually, she becomes incapable of fulfilling her responsibilities at home and finds it difficult to even care for her children. Every day her condition worsens.

Then suddenly one day she just snaps out of this state. She hadn't attended any church service or received any laying on of hands or taken any specific medication for her condition. She simply felt normal again. The torment that plagued her just went away on its own, leaving the wife relieved and released from its grip.

The next day she rises with a renewed sense of vitality and thinks, "Wow, I feel like mowing the grass and going for a run. I see my kids in a whole new light. Hello, husband! I love you!" It's as if she effortlessly returns to her normal state of mind, snapping back into reality. She thinks the dark days are long behind her, but what she doesn't realize is that a tormenting demon had simply chosen to leave her for reasons of his own.

Then one day the demon comes back and observes this positive transformation in her life and sarcastically says, "Oh, really? Torment vanished, nightmares gone, marriage on the mend, children thriving, and the house is clean and orderly. She even seems to have pulled herself together nicely." The demon finds the house as empty as when he left, and now it's swept clean and dressed up all pretty, but the door is still open to him.

Please take this to heart: if you leave your front door open long enough, something unwelcome is coming into your house. It's as true in the spiritual world as in the natural world. In the natural, it might be a mosquito or even a bear. It's a simple concept. If you leave your front door open, rest assured something will find its way inside. So, the demon in our allegory found its primary dwelling place vacant, tidied up, and adorned. The entire place had been cleaned up, and the front door stood wide open.

But as we read in verse 45 of Matthew 12, the demon then goes into the house and takes with himself seven demons more wicked than himself. From this we see he's still in control of the narrative.

He's never been evicted, nor has he been commanded out by any authority or asked not to return. So he proceeds to gather seven other spirits even more wicked than he is. It's as if he visits the demonic gathering spot and announces, "Hey, boys! Are you ready to party?" Then he selects other demons of greater malevolence than himself, and together they enter the house.

Demons can do this because the first demon still has legal rights through the gatekeeper to get in. The house remains under his control. In this allegory, please notice that the person has not gone through deliverance, so the demons can walk in and out at will. This is precisely why deliverance is necessary—to firmly and legally shut the door so they can't come back.

The Bible says demons enter of their own will "and *dwell there*." They literally live there night and day and make themselves at home. They are fluffing up the couch and turning on the big screen. But they're not just sitting around twiddling their thumbs. Oh, no; they're tormenting the person worse than before.

Now that the demon has returned with seven worse demons, the wife finds herself confined to her bed for days on end. She now becomes indifferent to her husband, her children, her pets, and her appearance. Her health deteriorates, leading to severe weight loss and constant nausea. Engaging in spiritual activities becomes increasingly challenging, while even watching preachers on YouTube triggers a nauseous response. The situation continues to worsen.

The first demon was never given an eviction notice, and now there are seven more who have the same legal rights. Consequently, they can freely come and go as they please while still maintaining ownership and control of the house. Future temporary departures of the demons may offer a short-lived sense of improvement, perhaps lasting a few days or even months. However, once the seven wicked spirits leave, each one—like the first—now has the potential to gather another seven more wicked than themselves and return. That's what I call "demonic compounded interest," with the intensity and influence of the demonic presence escalating exponentially over time.

Meanwhile, the wife's state of being has transitioned from relatively decent to completely subjugated and controlled by the demons over time. With each departure and return, the number of demons increases, further intensifying their hold over her. This cycle perpetuates the woman's worsening condition.

Please don't miss the urgency in this principle. First, it should inspire many people to realize they should never fear the possibility of returning demons, and even more to realize that their freedom from recurring bouts of heaviness or torment could be just a single deliverance session away. Second, we must realize that this cautionary teaching is intended to wake us to the reality that there is no other way to freedom except through Jesus. Demons may leave for a short while, making things appear to be getting better, but they will inevitably return, and things will only get worse.

If you think you or your loved ones can find freedom and spiritual healing without following Jesus' teachings on these subjects, you may find yourself in a pattern similar to that of the wife in our allegory. Never forget that deliverance is the children's bread and healing awaits all who desperately seek it (Matt. 15:21–28).

THIS WICKED GENERATION

> Then goeth he, and taketh with himself seven other spirits more wicked than himself, and they enter in and dwell there: and the last state of that man is worse than the first. Even so shall it be also unto this wicked generation.
>
> —JESUS (MATTHEW 12:45)

As we take another look at verse 45 of our key passage, we see that Jesus closes this message with the words, "Even so shall it be also unto this wicked generation." I used to think, "What does that have to do with demons?" I never really understood that in the past, so I tended to skip over it. But now that I understand this principle,

I've learned that it proves the great urgency for deliverance in the church.

Jesus said "this wicked generation" because the religious folks of His time refused to understand or embrace the concept of deliverance. Even more, as we learned in this chapter, they thought that act of casting out demons was a product of demonic influence. So with this statement Jesus highlighted their fundamental problem: by rejecting deliverance, they were allowing the demonic influence to multiply and intensify in their generation. Without the freedom and liberation that comes through deliverance, their wicked state could only further deteriorate as the demonic forces grew stronger and more pervasive every day.

Jesus was saying, in effect, "This condition of the man whose demons come and go as they please, growing seven times more wicked at will, is exactly how it will be for you."

There's a parallel that can be drawn to modern-day America. In 1995, the homosexual community said, "All we want is to be recognized." And Christians "in that generation" did nothing about it; they failed to take action. As a result, demons gained the right to free rein within the culture, coming and going and joining with even more companions over time. From 1995 to 2023, within the span of a single generation, we witnessed a dramatic shift. We went from hearing "We just want to be recognized" to coercive demands such as "If you don't use my pronoun, you will lose your job" and "Your kids will be subjected to drag queens in a public library that your tax dollars pay for, and you'll have no say."

So how did we arrive at this point from 1995 to 2023? The absence of genuine power and authority to drive out demons allowed a wicked generation to grow even more wicked. The demons freely came and went, resulting in the *demonic compounded interest* we saw in the allegory above. The demonic influence over our culture continues to escalate, and if we stay quiet for twenty more years, the consequences for our nation will be even more devastating. We have to take authority over the demons in Jesus' name, and that has to start with the church—the bride of Christ.

In the next chapter I'm going to continue exposing the works of demons, but before we move on, I want to be clear: my goal in this chapter was not to say that demons cannot ever come back to their host after being cast out, as there are definitely cases where they can. I simply needed to dispel a concern that has inadvertently instilled the fear in people that they need to be excessively cautious with deliverance. Some people believe that a single negative thought or a single stumble of some sort could result in the return of not only one but seven demons more wicked, even after five deliverance sessions. But that's simply not true.

The consequence of that kind of misguided preaching is that deliverance services have been filled with people who no longer need deliverance but are still in need of freedom from their *strongholds*. In the next chapter we will discuss strongholds, and I will identify when deliverance is needed and what is actually needed when deliverance is not.

> Therefore, as you received Christ Jesus the Lord, so walk in him, rooted and built up in him and established in the faith, just as you were taught, abounding in thanksgiving.
>
> —Colossians 2:6–7, esv

PART 3

FURTHER DEMYSTIFYING DELIVERANCE

Chapter 11

UNDERSTANDING CURSES
AND STRONGHOLDS

*And he said to man, "Behold, the fear of the Lord, that is
wisdom, and to turn away from evil is understanding."*

—JOB 28:28, ESV

DELIVERANCE MINISTRY ENCOMPASSES three distinct
aspects of spiritual warfare: casting out demons, dismantling strongholds, and breaking curses. Generational
curses, demons, and strongholds are three very different things,
and we have to approach them as three distinct facets of the enemy's arsenal against us. In short, demons are expelled through
deliverance, strongholds are brought down through discipline, and
curses are broken by decree.

In all three facets of deliverance ministry, that authority is given
by Jesus through the indwelling of the Holy Spirit. While a person
afflicted by demons or evil spirits requires deliverance—casting
the demons out in Jesus' name—those dealing with strongholds
must apply greater discipline to dismantle them. This chapter isn't
intended to teach all there is to know about curses and strongholds,
but I trust this review will equip you with more than enough understanding to start breaking and overcoming them in short order.

GENERATIONAL CURSES

There are two basic types of curses: those cast on people through a spoken word or some form of witchcraft and those passed on to people through their bloodline, which we call generational curses. We see generational curses defined in the Book of Exodus, where they're identified as "the iniquity of the fathers upon the children, and upon the children's children, unto the third and to the fourth generation" (34:7). To release a person from generational curses, you decree the curses to be broken.

A decree is simply a spoken order or command made with the full legal authority that all believers have in the name of Jesus. Before we go further, I want to make one thing clear about generational curses. When someone decrees that a person's generational curse has been broken, and that person agrees with the decree, the matter is resolved at that time. There is no need for them to keep decreeing that the same curse be broken numerous times. By coming into agreement with the decree, they have severed the legal covenant of the curse with the enemy, and the issue is settled once and for all.

Sometimes in deliverance ministry we revisit a previously broken curse in an attempt to break it again. By doing so, we're unintentionally imposing a belief that these curses still persist, inadvertently placing a new curse upon the very person we're trying to help! The curse will end because you have decreed it to end. But that doesn't mean you don't have to break new curses that may come against you (through some form of witchcraft) or gain the discipline to tear down the strongholds a generational curse may have patterned into your life. This "once and for all" breaking I am referring to is only for generational curses in your bloodline. Once you burn that altar, it's burned for good and the curses are rendered powerless.

OTHER CURSES

If someone bewitches you, curses you, or makes false prophecies against you, you absolutely have the ability to break free from those as well. In this discussion it's important to know the difference between someone cursing us with mere harsh words and someone persecuting us with a curse. The first type of cursing is what we commonly call "cussing," which may involve bashing people with harsh criticisms and other negative words. Though this is very common and far more benign, it still needs to be dealt with and avoided. This first type of cursing can easily turn into actual word curses when repeated without repentance or said with intent to persecute, so it should never be minimized or excused away.

In the previous chapter we saw where Jesus taught that an evil heart produces evil words, and that we will be judged for every idle and careless word we speak (Matt. 12:34–36). For this, even the most casual harsh language is considered evil by God. Jesus also said, "Those things which proceed out of the mouth come forth from the heart; and they defile the man" (Matt. 15:18), so if you are guilty of this type of cursing, you need to stop.

The Bible basically says that every word we speak is either a blessing or a curse, so we need to do all we can to tame our tongues, for they are "an unruly evil, full of deadly poison" (Jas. 3:8). Since first experiencing deliverance and being baptized in the Holy Spirit, when I received my prayer language, I have experienced a remarkable shift in my tongue. I've spent considerable time repenting for my past harsh words about people and movements I simply didn't know or understand. I trust I'm not alone in this regard.

In contrast to mere harsh words, we see in Matthew 5 that Jesus said, "Bless them that curse you." In this passage He was referring to a different kind of cursing from people who seek to "persecute you" (v. 44). These include word curses and other acts of witchcraft and sorcery. Of course, we again see His command to bless rather than strike back, but these types of curses do require faithful action in the Spirit.

When someone intentionally puts a curse on us, it's a whole new ball game. In such instances, in addition to breaking the curse through decree in faith, we can take a stronger stance and even take a higher level of response that isn't an act of retaliation but of defense. In fact, the Bible tells us we can in some cases reverse the curse to repel it, as Psalm 109:17 says, "As he loved cursing, so let it come unto him: as he delighted not in blessing, so let it be far from him." The Scriptures basically give us the right to tell those curses, "Return to sender," but we need to remember that this retribution will be carried out by the Lord and not by us.

THE POWER OF DISCIPLINE

A person with strongholds doesn't need more deliverance from demons; they need more discipline. Their ability to resist the sinful behaviors that have fortified that stronghold is paramount, and engaging in Bible reading, fasting, and prayer—including the daily putting on of the whole armor of God—will benefit them greatly. In the same way, by saying *no* to the temptations of the flesh through the authority of Jesus' name, they can effectively confront and weaken the strongholds in their life. We focused on the following passage from Matthew in the previous chapter, but I want you to read it again.

> When the unclean spirit is gone out of a man, he walketh through dry places, seeking rest, and findeth none. Then he saith, I will return into my house from whence I came out: and when he is come, he findeth it empty, swept, and garnished.
> —MATTHEW 12:43–44

Notice the words "my house." This is where we get to the nitty-gritty of strongholds, so please pay close attention. Demons fortify themselves in a person's life by building a house. The Bible calls that fortified place or city a stronghold. It's a house. It's a home. It's a habitation, a dwelling.

Here's where many folks miss a crucial aspect of deliverance. We wonder why people keep returning for the same issue when we have already cast that demon out numerous times, and when the people ask for more deliverance, we tend to go into full-blown deliverance ministry mode all over again.

But the truth is that you only need to expel that demon once. You cast it out in Jesus' name, you tell it not to come back, and from that very moment it is unequivocally banned from reentering that person's life. That's deliverance as Jesus did it, encapsulated into a single sentence. It really is that simple. The time involved can be different for everyone, which I'll discuss more toward the end of this chapter.

Though a demon has no choice but to eventually leave, that doesn't mean the person won't struggle afterward. They very well might. When a demon departs from the person, it leaves behind remnants of its house—what Derek Prince calls a nest, which is the comfortable place it built for itself. This is what we call a stronghold. While you can successfully cast the demon out, it is equally crucial to guide the person in the process of dismantling the stronghold—the nest—constructed by the enemy. That takes discipline, biblical obedience. Without cultivating discipline, the person will continue to feel like they are being plagued by a demon when in reality they mostly need to exercise self-control over their own desires and impulses.

Let me share a bit more of Derek Prince's very insightful perspective on this matter. He said the stronghold can be likened to a nest that the demons lived in before being expelled from a person. Therefore, if you address the demon but fail to deal with the nest, the stronghold remains intact. This is where the situation becomes complex and can get controversial. I'm not trying to identify a new doctrine. I'm just telling you the facts of my life experiences, and undoubtedly yours if you've had any experience with deliverance. When a demon is cast out, the stronghold can persist, especially if it is deeply ingrained within the person.

Pulling Down Strongholds

> For the weapons of our warfare are not carnal, but mighty
> through God to the pulling down of strong holds.
> —2 Corinthians 10:4

Although we drive demons out all the time, we only recently began to fully grasp the importance of tearing down the stronghold the demon left behind. For instance, when you cast out the spirit of sexual perversion, it's got to leave, but it's crucial to recognize that its departure does not automatically eliminate a person's struggle with pornography. In a culture where that temptation is as close as a cell phone, that stronghold is especially unrelenting. The ongoing struggle does not necessarily indicate the presence of a lingering demon but rather the persistence of a fortified spiritual dwelling—a stronghold that needs to be dismantled.

In this case, additional deliverance sessions are not what is needed. Instead, a greater focus on discipline and self-control is the answer. The stronghold will remain intact until the person makes intentional efforts to pull it down.

In 2 Corinthians 10:3, Paul says, "For though we walk in the flesh, we do not war after the flesh." This doesn't mean that we don't engage in warfare. Rather, it signifies that our battles are not fought using earthly, fleshly means. The nature of these struggles goes beyond the physical realm. They are supernatural battles. That's precisely why the Bible instructs us to put on the armor of God, which is not physical armor but spiritual. By doing so, we take a stand against the trickery of the devil in the spiritual realm that rules over the physical.

If you've already read *Weapons of Our Warfare*, this will be a bit of a review for you, but it's well worth it. Continuing in 2 Corinthians 10, notice the significant shift once this spirit is driven out. Verse 4 then states, "For the weapons of our warfare are not carnal, but mighty through God to the pulling down of strong holds." Did you realize that among all the armor of God, every bit of it except one piece is designed for defensive protection rather than direct offensive combat? That single essential combative weapon is revealed in Ephesians 6:17—the sword of the Spirit, which is the Word of God.

What does the shield of faith do? It quenches the wicked fiery darts that come against you. The shoes offer protection, the helmet guards your mind, the breastplate shields your heart, and the belt of truth secures your core. Each of these elements provides defense. There's only one piece that defends you with offensive force: God's chosen weapon, the Bible.

A stronghold is the result of someone or something imposing a strong influence and establishing a firm grip on your life, so to speak. In addition to demonic activity, this could manifest through various aspects of your life such as your relationships like your marriage, your thoughts, or even your diversions. So please take this to heart: once a stronghold is constructed, it doesn't require a demon to operate it because a person's flesh will move right in and get very comfortable within the nesting place that an evil spirit built within them. For that, we have to purposefully and consistently pull them down.

DEMOLISHING STRONGHOLDS

Again, when someone has genuinely undergone deliverance, the demons are gone, but it is essential that the person exercise discipline to deal with what the demons left behind. Yes, they have to legally close every door and ensure they don't backslide into a state that makes things even worse, but as we're learning, there is still work to be done in the Spirit. For this, it's crucial to understand the difference between deliverance and discipline.

Looking back at 2 Corinthians 10:4 again, notice it says our spiritual weapons are mighty "to the *pulling down* of strong holds" (emphasis added). Do you know what the original Greek word for *pulling down* means? It means *demolition*. It doesn't just mean you pull at it or neatly dismantle it. It means you *demolish* the house that the evil spirit left when you kicked it out—and that requires real biblical discipline.

The people who are still dealing with strongholds after deliverance haven't removed the triggers on their cell phones or on Netflix. They need to delete a few apps, lose a few phone numbers, or change their phone number altogether. Self-discipline requires exerting self-control, such as stepping away from the table and realizing that five chicken legs are enough! The examples go on and on, but you get the point. If you don't take decisive action to dismantle the strongholds in your life, they will inevitably worsen. This is why Paul exhorts us to crucify the flesh (Gal. 5:24). For inspiration, consider these well-known words Paul penned in his letter to the Galatians:

> I have been crucified with Christ. It is no longer I who live, but Christ who lives in me. And the life I now live in the flesh I live by faith in the Son of God, who loved me and gave himself for me.
>
> —GALATIANS 2:20, ESV

So, the demon comes out when you expel it, but the stronghold comes down when you demolish it. You must tear up that mess. Break it down. *Cast down* what the Bible calls "imaginations, and every high thing that exalteth itself" (2 Cor. 10:5). That means to cast down any harmful thoughts and every lofty notion that seeks to elevate itself above righteousness. I believe if you will immerse yourself in the Bible—the sword of the Spirit—you will beat that stronghold to death and utterly demolish it.

NOT A REVOLVING DOOR

So now we know. Deliverance ministry should never become a revolving door; not for the host nor for the ministry that cast it out. There should be no such thing as repeat customers. Either the deliverance has already taken place or it hasn't. True deliverance eradicates the demons, and anyone who questions this is actually questioning whether Jesus really gave us His authority as He claimed.

Once we have decreed the curses off people and confronted their demons in Jesus' name, it's simply time for them to take personal responsibility and get disciplined. It is imperative to get into the Word, make wise choices, and learn to say no to certain things— and say yes to others. As emphasized in Matthew 17:21, where we see Jesus cast out an especially difficult demon, prayer and fasting are essential skills to acquire.

I want to clarify that I'm not denying the possibility of an evil spirit ever returning if someone reopens the door by entering into a new legal contract with a demon through repetitive unrepentant sin. That should be obvious even to a new convert. However, the notion that ongoing struggles automatically mean you are still plagued by demons is a lie from hell. It's a false doctrine that has trapped people in theological bondage. I've learned that this is the primary reason people have a hard time accepting deliverance ministry. As we learned in the previous chapter, the religious spirit is always at work trying to keep people in bondage through blasphemies and false doctrines.

You might be reading this book right now after having gone through deliverance, and you're still battling an addiction. Are you willing to spend the next ten years screaming, "Spirit of *pharmakeia*, come out"? When the demon was cast out and the door was closed in Jesus' name, what you needed next was an honest transformation of your mindset and lifestyle, not more deliverance. You must undergo a renewal of your inner spirit by walking in the Spirit and refusing to walk in the flesh any longer. If you still struggle after deliverance, it does not mean you haven't been delivered. It doesn't mean you're lost either. The struggle is proof of who you are in Christ. Lost people don't struggle with sin in the same way. We simply must take control of our flesh and its passions and desires.

> But I say, walk by the Spirit, and you will not gratify the desires of the flesh. For the desires of the flesh are against the Spirit, and the desires of the Spirit are against the flesh, for these are opposed to each other, to keep you from doing the things you want to do.

> —Galatians 5:16–17, esv

It may surprise some people that one of the works of the flesh, as clearly stated in Galatians 5:20, is witchcraft. It's interesting that some people claim they don't believe a Christian can be influenced by a demon, yet the reality is that someone's flesh can generate behaviors akin to witchcraft. It doesn't get much more influenced or "demonized" than that, and it's happening in the flesh, not the spirit. The Bible states it plainly: in our flesh dwells no good thing (Rom. 7:18).

I am absolutely committed to spending my life casting out demons. However, if I'm to feed the sheep, I must also spend my life teaching people how to be disciplined and make wise choices—saying yes to the right things and saying no to the wrong things. That's what the Word of God teaches.

When Deliverance Isn't Instantaneous

It's important to recognize that not all deliverances are quick, and not all of them are overwhelming. As noted earlier, the deliverance process may require longer durations for some. I've witnessed instant deliverance, but I've also taken part in sessions that lasted many hours. As a deliverance minister becomes more adept at discerning spirits, it's possible to condense a five-hour deliverance session into just fifteen minutes, but we see no set time span in the Bible.

The misconception that all deliverance is instantaneous has become a widespread problem, even among my preacher friends. They often mention how Jesus simply spoke a word and the demons promptly departed. But that's not entirely accurate.

In Mark chapter 5 the Bible explicitly states that the demons resisted Jesus. In one of the most dramatic examples of deliverance in action, Jesus dealt with a crying, begging demon that "besought him much" (v. 10), and only God knows how long that lasted. The word *much* describes the intensity of their actions. It signifies that Jesus had to persistently engage with these troublesome entities for an extended period of time.

Let's consider what happened when Paul encountered the girl with a spirit of divination in Acts 16. He simply said, "Come out of her," and the Bible records that the spirit left her that very hour. There was no complicated process or ambiguity, so sometimes things can be incredibly straightforward. However, when the demonic influence is deeply entrenched, a more thorough approach is necessary. Ultimately, we need to stop overcomplicating things, regardless of the time it takes to help a person find freedom. While deliverance ministry is so simple that it shouldn't work, I've learned that it works because it is so simple. There's power in the mighty name of Jesus. That's the bottom line.

I give praise to God for the vital ministry of deliverance, but I also recognize the significance of ongoing Christian discipleship. Without a doubt, I firmly believe in the reality of demons and the fact that they need to be effectively addressed in the name of Jesus. However, I equally believe in the importance of spiritual discipline and the continual renewing of your mind and heart with the Word of God.

There is a phrase that computer technicians often use: "garbage in, garbage out," or GIGO for short. Simply put, if we input garbage into a computer, we can only expect garbage output. Likewise, as Christians, by immersing ourselves in the right things, we will naturally displace the wrong things while producing the right things.

So let's adapt "GIGO" to say "BIBO": "Bible in, Bible out." Once we fill ourselves with the Word of God, it will overflow in our lives, permeating every aspect. As we'll learn in the next chapter, that's something we should be desperate for.

> Your words were found, and I ate them, and your words became to me a joy and the delight of my heart, for I am called by your name, O LORD, God of hosts.
> —JEREMIAH 15:16

Chapter 12

THE POWER OF DESPERATION

The wise men are ashamed, they are dismayed and taken: lo,
they have rejected the word of the LORD; and what wisdom
is in them? Therefore will I give their wives unto others, and
their fields to them that shall inherit them: for every one from
the least even unto the greatest is given to covetousness, from
the prophet even unto the priest every one dealeth falsely.
—JEREMIAH 8:9–10

NOW THAT WE know there is still work to be done after deliverance, it's important to recognize the power of desperation—desperation for deliverance and for the Word of God. For that, I want to take a look at the Book of Jeremiah, which is one of the strangest theological books in the entire Bible.

Jeremiah was called by the Lord at age fifteen to preach for forty-plus years to a nation that did not give one flip of a wooden nickel about anything he said. Only a handful of people were true-blue converts of the message Jeremiah had to preach, and that message was not a casual "just come to the Lord and all your dreams will be fulfilled" kind of message. He preached a message of deep repentance and thundered out the truth of the Word to a rebellious group of people that sat there bug-eyed and hard-hearted and refused to listen.

For more than four decades Jeremiah smashed strongholds, fought devils, and called the people away from the bondage of iniquity and idolatry. In Jeremiah 8, he's still in the introduction of his lifelong sermon of repentance. Here's a man who was thrown into a miry pit—not just a prison with "three hots and a cot," but a literal pit of mud and stench—on two occasions for preaching the Word. Later in the narrative we see Jeremiah become so discouraged that he said, "O LORD, you have deceived me" (Jer. 20:7, ESV). Have you ever felt deceived by God? Have you ever felt like God gave you a promise and it didn't come to pass when you thought it should?

Jeremiah eventually got so discouraged that he was tempted to walk away from the things of God, "but his word was in mine heart as a burning fire shut up in my bones, and I was weary with forbearing, and I could not stay" (20:9). No matter how rebellious the people were, no matter how discouraged he became, he couldn't quit because the word of God was boiling and stirring in him—and it wouldn't let him go.

Jeremiah was one of the few true prophets left in the southern kingdom of Judah after the nation of Israel split into two kingdoms. The king was a fleshly puppet. The priests had corrupted themselves. The prophets had polluted themselves because they were all about the money. Their ministry was no longer about the manifested glory of God or the truth. It was about being seen by men instead of being exalted by God and used for the glory of His message. They cared about the manifestation of their own lives, not the manifestation of the power of God.

In Jeremiah 8, something happened that I've read more than a hundred times, but for some reason I never caught it until we got a glimpse of what God was teaching us on this journey of deliverance. In the passage at the top of this chapter, we see that the wise men began to be ashamed of the word of the Lord. In response, God said, "I'm going to kill all of you." That's what He means when He says, "I'm going to give your wives to others and your land to those that shall inherit it." (See verse 10.) He said, "I'm going to judge you and wipe you off the face of the earth. You've been rebellious far too long, and you've been preaching something that is not true. And because of that, My people have no healing."

HEALED *SLIGHTLY*

> For they have healed the hurt of the daughter of my people slightly, saying, Peace, peace; when there is no peace.
> —JEREMIAH 8:11

This seems like such a strange place to talk about deliverance; but watch closely. Those who knew the truth—the prophets and the priests—were responsible to share the truth, but they did not. Thus, they were under the judgment of God, as are so many of the false prophets of our day. Why? Verse 11 (above) gives us the answer. Notice that word *slightly*. The phrase "the daughter of my people" is generational terminology. God is saying that Jeremiah's generation had been healed *somewhat* by the message, and it mirrors exactly what we are living right now in the American church. When the manifested power of God begins to explode in our midst, we try to explain it away because it doesn't fit the denominational narrative of how we were raised. It doesn't go through the lens of how we were taught to read the Bible.

This is the most disparaging remark that could be said of these people: "They have healed the hurt of the daughter of my people *slightly*" (emphasis added). The priests gave the people just enough to keep them coming. They cranked up the music just enough to get the people bopping and jamming. They prayed just enough prayers not to make the people too uncomfortable. They preached just long enough to make the people feel like they had been to a motivational pop psychology meeting—so they could walk in the doors feeling one way and walk out feeling better about themselves, never learning anything about the glory of God.

As we've pressed into this journey of deliverance at Global Vision

CAST IT OUT

and everywhere we preach, I've discovered that my eyes had been purposely closed to things I refused to take notice of because of the discomfort they brought. And like the people of Jeremiah's day, most believers today have experienced a degree of deliverance—*slightly*. They have a degree of sanctification—*slightly*. People have walked the aisle, signed a card, and prayed a prayer, but they've only been set free *slightly* because they're still in bondage to their past. You will never be delivered from what is attacking you and oppressing you until you get desperate for the deliverance you need from God.

NOT SUPPOSED TO BE NATURAL

We've raised a generation of fortune-cookie Christians who are looking for a Jesus that gives them whatever they want. If the Bible says we can be filled with joy and filled with peace and filled with power, then why do we come to church and feel so distracted? It's because we're filled with things we want in the flesh. It's because we've been healed slightly.

People say, "Oh, we're saved by the grace of God," but some of you are addicted to pornography because you've only been healed slightly. "I've got victory in Jesus"—but you can't get away from the bottle because you've been healed slightly. The Bible says, in effect, "The priests and prophets gave them just enough truth to get out of some trouble, but they were only healed slightly." And that's where we are in the church today. We have just enough truth to feel a little better—at times—but we're still in bondage and we still have strongholds. The church has only been healed slightly because most aren't desperate for the things of God and dead religion has taken His place at the altar. That's why people can come to church, hear a good message, make a glorious decision, and—though they might feel better in the moment—still go home unchanged. Without desperation, they're only healed slightly.

Even though the Holy Spirit indwells the holy of holies in our

146

body, there are still demonizing spirits that try to destroy the work of the Spirit within us. The church in America is in a floundering mess: Sicknesses that could be healed. Children that could be set free. Marriages that could be restored. Strongholds like addictions and bondages that could be demolished. Religion that could be shattered—all with a proper understanding of what the Bible truly says about each. It's a supernatural work of a supernatural God through a supernatural book. It's not supposed to be *natural,* and that's why it bothers us.

So we cry "peace, peace," but there is no peace. We say "everything's good" while the Father's house is burning to the ground. We as the church just stay in our sin. We stay in our rebellion. We stay in our lust. We stay in our addiction. We stay bound up in the strongholds of the enemy's making. If you struggle with these and still say, "It's all good," you're wrong. It's not! The devil has a foothold in your life, and the things you're struggling with need to be renounced in the name of Jesus. You need to get desperate for deliverance!

Pentecost Continued

> And it shall come to pass afterward, that I will pour out my spirit upon all flesh; and your sons and your daughters shall prophesy, your old men shall dream dreams, your young men shall see visions: And also upon the servants and upon the handmaids in those days will I pour out my spirit. And I will shew wonders in the heavens and in the earth, blood, and fire, and pillars of smoke. The sun shall be turned into darkness, and the moon into blood, before the great and terrible day of the Lord come.
>
> —Joel 2:28–31

The fulfillment of this passage from Joel 2 began on the day of Pentecost as recorded in Acts 2, and it is still being fulfilled to this day. This degree of outpouring will not go away until the sun is darkened and the moon is turned into blood on that great and ter-rible day of the Lord (v. 31). We know that Pentecost is still flowing today in the church because this "great and terrible day" has yet to arrive. This outpouring out of God's Spirit on "all flesh" will con-tinue all the way to the end of days when the greatest harvesting revival on the planet is going to take place. These are *those* days.

> And it shall come to pass, that whosoever shall call on the name of the LORD shall be delivered: for in mount Zion and in Jerusalem shall be deliverance, as the LORD hath said, and in the remnant whom the LORD shall call.
>
> —JOEL 2:32

In this concluding verse of Joel 2 the prophet tells us that from Pentecost to the end times—*now*—whosoever shall call on the name of the Lord shall be *delivered*. The parallel reference to this prophecy in Acts 2 reads, "And it shall come to pass, that who-soever shall call on the name of the Lord shall be *saved*" (v. 21, emphasis added), so salvation is deliverance. The promise of this great revival is not one of bigger crowds but of greater deliverance of God's people—the remnant who are desperate enough to call on Jesus' name with purpose, no longer seeking deliverance *slightly* but in spirit and in truth (John 4:24).

This passage in Joel has been in the Bible all along—through all my days in seminary and all my days of preaching—but I just didn't have the spiritual capacity to accept its deepest meaning until now. As Joel reveals, this last-days deliverance shall be in Zion and Jerusalem, "and in the remnant whom the LORD shall call." For this we know the remnant church will be marked by deliverance.

I've been known as a preacher who is baptized in boldness, and as our people at Global Vision have proven, this sort of courage is contagious. We are a remnant church. There is no doubt about that. If we can stand so boldly in life and in death in the face of this buck-wild culture, shouldn't we be equally as bold if not bolder with the truth of the Word of God when it comes across our eyes and gets planted in our hearts and minds? The answer is yes. We are submitting to the Word of God. We're desperate for it. When the Word of God and a supernatural experience meet and God confirms His Word to the hearts of His children, they simply obey. These are the markers of the remnant people who are called by God in these last of the last days.

> So too at the present time there is a remnant, chosen by grace.
> —ROMANS 11:5, ESV

Chapter 13

OVERCOMING THE ENEMY

And I heard a loud voice saying in heaven, Now is come salva-
tion, and strength, and the kingdom of our God, and the power
of his Christ: for the accuser of our brethren is cast down, which
accused them before our God day and night. And they over-
came him by the blood of the Lamb, and by the word of their
testimony; and they loved not their lives unto the death.
—REVELATION 12:10–11

DESPITE THE HARDSHIPS it presented, many of which still persist today, the national disaster that started in 2020 was a gift to the body of Christ. The COVID debacle didn't *cause* problems in the church; it *exposed* the problems that had been there for decades. Before 2020 many of us would hear things about the coming "beast" system, the Antichrist, and a one-world currency and think those events were hundreds of years away, but we are now watching the Word of God be fulfilled before our very eyes.

In a matter of twenty-four months we jumped fifty years pro-phetically in this nation. So lift up your eyes, because your redemp-tion draws nigh! Jesus Christ is coming again! It's time we all figure out which side we're on because God is drawing a line in the sand. The Word of God and the culture are on a collision course, and you cannot follow Jesus and the culture at the same time. With that fact firmly in hand, it's crucial for the body to understand the prophetic role of deliverance in these last days. I briefly addressed the key passage above earlier in the book, but let's take a deeper look at its revelatory message.

The Book of Revelation is both a historical and a prophetic narrative, meaning that some events in it have been fulfilled and some have not yet taken place. In it we frequently see the *double reference principle* in action. Our passage above offers a prime example. The apostle John is referring to the fall of Satan from heaven, as discussed in Ezekiel 28 and Isaiah 14, but he's also referring to what is going to happen when the last-day saints stand against the authority of the Antichrist. In Revelation 12:11 the apostle John, also known as *John the Revelator*, tells us how we will ultimately overcome the devil through a simple prescription, and it all starts with the power in the precious blood of the Lamb of God!

The blood of Jesus has provided two things for everyone. First, it has provided us with atonement. Second, it brought us into oneness with God. As a result, we are seen as perfect children in the eyes of God. Practically, we're still a mess, but positionally, we're heaven bound as if we were already there. The Book of Ephesians says we are seated with Christ in heavenly places (2:6) and that we're accepted in the beloved (1:6) all because He who knew no sin became sin for us, that we might be made the righteousness of God in Him (2 Cor. 5:21). Jesus is not one of multiple ways to the kingdom; He's the one and only way to the kingdom.

As we continue in Revelation 12:11, we also see that we overcome the devil by *the word* of our *testimony*. The Bible is saying, "Let the redeemed of the Lord say so" (Ps. 107:2)! You've got to tell people what God did for you—that's the word of your testimony—because they can't deny what you've experienced. They can argue about church music, they can argue about the big screens, they can argue about your clothes, but they can never argue about what you know the Holy Spirit did for you when you got born again.

THE REAL COST

In the final phrase of Revelation 12:11 we see the real cost of following Jesus in this victory: "They loved not their lives unto the death." When Jesus showed up on the scene and started preaching and healing and setting the captives free through deliverance, everybody said, "We're going to follow You, Lord, anywhere and everywhere." Jesus responded, in effect, "Oh, I doubt it, because foxes have holes, and the birds of the air have nests, but the Son of Man has no place to even lay His head." (See Luke 9:58.)

When Jesus heard emotionally charged promises of lifelong devotion from His disciples, He would spin around and give them the most abrasive challenges that ever fell from human lips. He would look them square in the face and say things like, "You want to follow Me? Here's what you do: hate your father, hate your mother, hate your wife, hate your brother, and hate your sister. Hate your own life also, or you cannot be My disciple." (See Luke 14:26.)

Was the loving God of the universe telling us to hate people? No, He wasn't telling us to hate anyone. On the contrary. In that particular statement Jesus was using *comparative terminology*, comparing two things in hyperbolic fashion to make one very emphatic theological point.

He's not telling us to hate our family. He's telling us we should love Him so much that our love for anyone else—spouse and children included—would seem like hatred in comparison. So, in our key passage, He's putting our love of life on the same scale.

We've raised a generation of people who use Christian lingo and say they would die for their faith, but most of them won't even go to church for their faith. We've raised a generation of people who love to talk about dying for a Jesus they don't even live for. In the context of our key passage, He's not asking you to die. He's asking you to live. He wants you to live for Him. The fact of the matter is we will never die for a Jesus that we don't live for every single day of our lives, consistently and faithfully. Scripture says, "Moreover it is required in stewards, that a man be found faithful" (1 Cor. 4:2). That's what God wants.

The last-days saints overcome the enemy because they understand the authority they walk in by the blood of the Lamb. They are unstoppable until God is done with them. They know that if they just share their testimony and, like the psalmist, cry out, "I waited patiently for the LORD; and he inclined unto me, and heard my cry. He brought me up also out of an horrible pit, out of the miry clay, and set my feet upon a rock, and established my goings. And he hath put a new song in my mouth, even praise unto our God: many shall see it, and fear, and shall trust in the LORD" (Ps. 40:1–3), souls will be saved.

There's nothing more powerful than the gospel and our testimony. Romans 1:16 says, "I am not ashamed of the gospel of Christ." If we're not ashamed of it, then we ought to be willing to live for it—and die for it, if need be. We don't see that kind of commitment in the church today because people are bending to the culture. They're looking to see what the latest church growth methodology is. They're blown and tossed about by every wind of doctrine. They heap to themselves teachers having itching ears, and they've turned their hearts away from the truth and turned unto fables.

Most people would rather watch a Disney cartoon in church than hear a man of God stand up and say, "This is what the Bible says." From the days of the prophets of the Old Testament through every great revival since the Pentecost, leather-lunged men of God have stood up and said, "The culture is wrong, but the Word of the Lord is right"—and they were willing to live and die by it.

Do you know what the Bible teaches? Follow Jesus, and it may not turn out so hot for you in the end. All the disciples except John died martyrs' deaths. Yet we somehow have this idea that we get to go through life with no problems whatsoever. The Bible clearly tells us that all who "live godly in Christ Jesus shall suffer persecution" (2 Tim. 3:12)—not because we're looking for it, but because persecution will find us if we're truly His.

If we are going to have victory, then we must do what the Bible says to do in order to get that victory. We need to overcome the enemy consistently through the gospel and our testimony as we walk in the power of Jesus Christ—as we walk in the anointing of the Holy Spirit with the authority of God's holy Word. We need to have victory over our flesh, victory over this culture, victory over the world, and victory over the devil. And the prescription is, "They overcame him by the blood of the Lamb, and by the word of their testimony" (Rev. 12:11).

THE BLOOD OF THE LAMB

> For it is not possible that the blood of bulls and of goats should take away sins.
>
> —HEBREWS 10:4

People are correct when they say the thirty-nine books of the Old Testament are a bloodbath. God has always required blood. But in the Old Testament, the blood sacrifice only covered up the sin and rebellion of the people, and it only covered their sin and rebellion for a limited period of time before another sacrifice would be required. Hebrews 9:22 tells us that without the shedding of blood there is no remission of sins, and before Jesus, this shedding of blood was required continually. There could never be enough blood sacrifice placed on that altar. The only word the altar knew was *sacrifice*. Then Jesus came as the fulfillment of the Old Testament—the ultimate blood sacrifice for the remission of all sin.

When John the Baptist watched Jesus approach him in the Jordan River to be baptized, he cried out at the top of his lungs, "Behold the Lamb of God, which taketh away the sin of the world" (John 1:29). Did you catch that? Jesus *taketh away* sin, not *covereth up* sin for the time being, as we see in the Old Testament. If your sins are taken away, that means they're gone for good.

> But if we walk in the light, as he is in the light, we have fellowship one with another, and the blood of Jesus Christ his Son cleanseth us from all sin.
>
> —1 John 1:7

When Jesus died on the cross and the veil was torn from top to bottom, it was God coming to man, not man working his way to God. The veil was rent, and Jesus said, "It is finished; it is done." You don't add to that truth; you don't subtract from it; you don't divide or multiply—it is done. The great transaction is accomplished! At that moment, when Jesus did for us what we had no capability of doing for ourselves, after thousands of years the altar learned a new word. All it knew before was *sacrifice, sacrifice, sacrifice.* But when Jesus finished the work of the gospel through the shedding of His blood, the altar learned a word that would last for all time: *satisfied, satisfied, satisfied.* No more sacrifices for sins!

THE POWER IN THE BLOOD

The blood of Jesus brought us unity with God and broke down the middle wall of partition so that we could walk right into His presence. We don't need to have a pastor, pope, president, or priest mediate for us because the blood of Jesus has made us kings and priests unto our God. Not only does the blood of Jesus give us unity with God but it also gives us authority over the devil, over demons, and over everything concerning us. There is power in the blood of Jesus and power in His name!

Many Christians today live as if the power of Jesus' name has diminished over the last two thousand years. It hasn't. Yet we have people by the thousands saying we are a bunch of heretics who have lost our minds because we walk in the supernatural power of God and set people free through deliverance. They say that was a different dispensation that is no longer in effect. To that I ask, when did the name of Jesus stop being powerful in any dispensation?

If you were to deal with somebody who is oppressed or in active addiction or a victim of full-blown demonic possession (yes, it still happens) and walk up to them and say, "In the name of Buddha, come out," you'll get spit on. Or if you say, "In the name of Confucius, come out," he isn't moving. There is only one name that has the authority to make the devils flee, and that's the name of the Lord Jesus Christ.

Revelation 12:11 gives us a simple prescription that proves the Great Commission of Christ. Until the very end of the Bible's prophetic narrative, believers will always have the power to cast out devils in Jesus' name—by the blood of the Lamb and the word of our testimony. Demons are everywhere, and people are in bondage to them, but very few believers are working to set them free. Is it any wonder the church and the nations are in such a demonized mess?

God has given us authority, and the American church should be walking in it rather than sitting around twiddling their thumbs while Rome is burning all around us. The Bible says in Mark 16:17, "These signs shall follow them *that believe*" (emphasis added), not "these signs shall follow them *that are ordained*." Jesus gave His commission to every believer, you and your family included. It's a tragedy that the church finds it so easy to love Mark 16:15 (NKJV), "Go into all the world and preach the gospel," but won't even acknowledge the call to set people free just two verses later. There is power in the name of Jesus, and Jesus told us to cast out devils under that authority. Why would we leave so much power and authority sitting on a shelf or tucked away in our back pockets?

We've got to armor up, church. We've got to suit up and boot up. This is not a Sunday school lesson. We're in a literal war against the rulers of the darkness of this world—against spiritual wickedness in high places (Eph. 6:12)—and the souls of the children of God are at stake.

THERE IS NO GOING BACK

James 4:7 says, "Submit yourselves therefore to God. Resist the devil, and he will flee from you." That's deliverance in short form. The devil came to steal, kill, and destroy, so if he has hold of something we care about, we gave it to him. The church has abdicated its biblical responsibility, operating as if we don't have the authority to fight back, but we clearly do. We've been trained in the American church to just show up and have a cute little service whether God shows up or not, but that is no longer acceptable.

The saints of God who have awakened to the full message of the Great Commission are deciding they're never going back to lukewarm religion, even if the only way forward is death. They're fighting tooth and nail against the enemy, against their flesh, against demonic oppression, against the perversity of this culture, and against the godlessness that we see rising in the world. If the gates of hell shall not prevail against us (Matt. 16:18), then you can be sure that this present darkness doesn't stand a chance against those of us who are washed in the blood of Jesus, willing to go down swinging for the gospel. We must resist.

> Beloved, when I gave all diligence to write unto you of the common salvation, it was needful for me to write unto you, and exhort you that ye should earnestly contend for the faith which was once delivered unto the saints.
>
> —JUDE 3

Chapter 14

DISCERNING OF SPIRITS

Now the Spirit speaketh expressly, that in the latter
times some shall depart from the faith, giving heed
to seducing spirits, and doctrines of devils;
—1 TIMOTHY 4:1

S WE TURN toward the end of this book, it's critically important that we sharpen our ability to discern evil spirits and their workings. For this, having the gift of *discerning of spirits* is especially valuable. Don't ever doubt that we all have to develop this discernment, especially when working in deliverance ministry. In this spiritual war, the discerning of spirits is the tip of the sword.

In the verse above, the apostle Paul is writing to his spiritual son, Timothy, to give him a picture of the spiritual warfare at hand. Be reminded that the "latter times" that Paul references in this verse began at Pentecost and continues through today. Paul was living in the beginning of the last days when he said these words almost two thousand years ago. Now when people ask, "You've been saying that Jesus is going to return for two thousand years; where are all the signs of His coming? Where is He?" I always respond, "If you read the Bible, you'll realize that it took Him four thousand years to show up the first time." True as that is, the prophetic timeline is suddenly accelerating at a startling rate, so we'd better buckle up.

In our key verse, where Paul refers to those who "shall depart from the faith," he is not talking about ungodly individuals who stick their middle finger in God's face, spit on the Bible, and hate church. He is talking about believers who will depart from the church, from the truth of the Bible, from the preaching, from prayer, from fasting, and from deliverance and miracles. And the reason they will depart is shocking: they will give heed to seducing spirits. This, of course, is not a reference to the Holy Spirit that is spoken of in the first part of the verse. These are evil spirits, and these dark seducing spirits will eventually woo them into accepting "doctrines of devils."

Doctrines of devils are false religions and other false teachings that dismiss the Bible: idol worship, the worship of man, the worship of objects, the worship of statues, the worship of beads, the worship of charms and amulets and crystals and horoscopes, etc.; and they will eventually defend every sort of perversion that goes against the Word of God. Church people will literally side with demons and occultism and witchcraft. If you haven't seen that come full circle in our time, then you haven't been paying attention. In short, Paul says there will be demonic activity in the church during the last days that will destroy the church.

> Speaking lies in hypocrisy; having their conscience seared with a hot iron; forbidding to marry, and commanding to abstain from meats, which God hath created to be received with thanksgiving of them which believe and know the truth.
> —1 TIMOTHY 4:2–3

I love the poetic nature of the King James Bible, but it often reads so poetically that we miss the point *practically*—yet the point is still there. In the last phrase of our initial key verse in 1 Timothy (verse 1, at the top of this chapter), notice that the phrase "doctrines of devils" ends with a semicolon, not a period. That means the thought continues into the next verse. But most people read the following verses (verses 2–3 above) in a way that lays all of this on the people: "Speaking lies in hypocrisy; having their conscience seared with a hot iron...."

There was a time when I read this scripture entirely out of its proper context. It's not actually the people who are forbidding to marry, whose consciences are seared, and who are speaking lies but the dark spirits inside those people causing them to do things they would not naturally do. The demons are causing them to speak lies and hypocrisy through the manipulation of their seduction and their doctrines of devils.

The influence of demonic activity in the life of the American church is an absolute fact, and through all my efforts to battle against it, I've discovered you cannot appeal to the conscience of a demon. It works to destroy the conscience of its host and has no conscience of its own. A demonic spirit is void of that emotional connection to God, so it causes people to live numb and dry and lukewarm and barren. In this context we begin to understand that a demon is nothing more than a person without a body who has taken hold of a human body.

When the Bible says, "We wrestle not against flesh and blood" (Eph. 6:12), it literally means "we do not wrestle with people that have bodies, but with those that do not have bodies of their own." Why do we think demons want to invade and oppress people? Because they need a body to carry out their diabolical behavior. In contrast, the spirits from God never invade people's bodies. Instead, they show up for the purpose of warfare and protection, and they always bring glory to God. Demons want to bring glory to themselves.

Known by Its Fruit

Either make the tree good and its fruit good, or make the tree bad and its fruit bad, for the tree is known by its fruit.
—Jesus (Matthew 12:33, esv)

Jesus delivered this famous quote immediately after being accused of casting out a demon by the power of Satan, as discussed earlier in this book. With it, aside from rebuking the Pharisees for blaspheming the Holy Spirit, He was teaching the importance of proper spiritual judgment and discernment.

As previously noted, the gift of the Spirit that is the most needed in deliverance ministry is the *discerning of spirits* (1 Cor. 12:10). While not everyone has this invaluable gift at its highest operating level, many of us have some degree of this gift, and all of us can discern the most telling signs of a demonic presence. We can most readily do this through the recognition of the bad fruit detailed in our key passage that is the product of seducing spirits and doctrines of demons—lying, hypocrisy, and a seared conscience being chief among them. Likewise, as Paul points out in his letter to the Galatians, the bad fruit that is *the works of the flesh* are evident:

Now the works of the flesh are evident: sexual immorality, impurity, sensuality, idolatry, sorcery, enmity, strife, jealousy, fits of anger, rivalries, dissensions, divisions, envy, drunkenness, orgies, and things like these. I warn you, as I warned you before, that those who do such things will not inherit the kingdom of God.
—Galatians 5:19–21, esv

As detailed in chapter 11 concerning strongholds, while not every work of the flesh is a spirit, Paul's outline here in Galatians is difficult to discount as the work of darkness, especially when these works are consistently "evident" in their practice. As Paul sternly warns, "those who do such things will not inherit the kingdom of

God" (v. 21, ESV). Surely any work that threatens your place in the kingdom of God is demonic, so if you're suffering from any of these, please get right with God and seek deliverance ministry immediately. The subject of our inheritance of the kingdom of God is far too complex to start discussing here, but I promise to dive deep into it in a future text. Suffice it to say in this book, you don't want to do any of these works of the flesh—or any other things like these.

In direct contrast, Paul also details the fruit of the Spirit in the very next verse of Galatians:

> But the fruit of the Spirit is love, joy, peace, patience, kindness, goodness, faithfulness, gentleness, self-control; against such things there is no law. And those who belong to Christ Jesus have crucified the flesh with its passions and desires.
> —GALATIANS 5:22–24, ESV

Surely, where the fruit of the Spirit is consistent and evident, it is far easier to discern that an evil spirit is *not* at work. "For the desires of the flesh are against the Spirit, and the desires of the Spirit are against the flesh, for these are opposed to each other, to keep you from doing the things you want to do" (Gal. 5:17, ESV). Again, if you struggle with the works of the flesh and find it difficult to consistently walk in the Spirit, you should seek deliverance ministry immediately.

TESTING THE SPIRITS

> Beloved, do not believe every spirit, but test the spirits to see whether they are from God, for many false prophets have gone out into the world.
> —1 JOHN 4:1, ESV

In this verse, the apostle John exhorts us to "test the spirits." When the Bible tells us to measure whether or not a spirit is "from God," that means some spirits are *of God* and all other spirits are not of

God. John is saying that the effort to avoid being seduced by the dark spirits in false prophets must involve testing the spirits, which points to the difficulty in discerning spirits that can appear as "angel[s] of light" (2 Cor. 11:14). We will often need to weigh spirits to discern whether they are angels of God or demons of Satan.

Hebrews 1:7 tells us, "He makes his angels winds, and his ministers a flame of fire" (ESV). Where angels minister to us, demons seek to destroy our peace. Aside from the goal of invading our flesh, that's the clearest mission of a demon. That's why you have depression (heaviness), anxiety, family issues, sickness, and disease. The devil wants to steal your peace. The angels of God have one job: they minister peace by coming to us in times of need.

The Bible says in Matthew 4 that after Jesus' forty-day confrontation with the devil, "angels came and ministered unto him" (v. 11). If Jesus needed to have angels minister to Him in times of need, how much more do we need angels to minister to us? In short, while angels minister peace to us and around us, demons steal peace from our flesh and from the atmosphere.

To further aid in discerning between angels and demons, it's important to recognize that there is never a time in the Bible that the angels require glory, praise, or worship. In fact, when people would fall down before the angels, the angels would say, "Stand up and worship God." But a demon wants to be worshipped and desires attention. While the gift of the discerning of spirits can and will expose them before they can go too far, we have to realize that demons are relentless, so remaining suited up in the whole armor of God is crucial in spiritual warfare. As we discuss in great detail in *Weapons of Our Warfare*, this Holy Spirit–powered arsenal should always remain our first line of defense.

I am convinced that we are in the battle of our lifetime as we do our gospel best to bring deliverance front and center for all the world to see—regardless of the discomfort it may cause. Demons relentlessly work against all of us, and it's foolish to ignore that fact. I am also convinced that we would be far more vulnerable while standing toe to toe with the enemy if it were not for the ministering spirits of God that have been loosed to protect us, encourage us, enlighten us, enrich us, and go before us in battle.

Angels are very real and often present, praise God. Do not allow yourself to get overwhelmed by the persistent workings of darkness, but rather recognize the far more powerful angels that are at work all around you, even when you are unaware (Heb. 13:2). Above all, stand firm in the armor of God through the indwelling of the Holy Spirit in the mighty name of Jesus!

> Besides this you know the time, that the hour has come for you to wake from sleep. For salvation is nearer to us now than when we first believed. The night is far gone; the day is at hand. So then let us cast off the works of darkness and put on the armor of light.
> —ROMANS 13:11–12, ESV

A BRUTALLY BEAUTIFUL JOURNEY

Looking back over the journey Global Vision has been on for the past few years, I have to be honest: it's been a crazy ride down the narrow road. We went from thinking deliverance was heretically abnormal to realizing—upon a clear reading of the New Testament—it is foundational to Christianity. In the Book of Acts they would preach the Word and demons would get so stirred up they would identify themselves. Then the preacher would simply say, "In the name of Jesus Christ you must come out," and it would just work—and the people's lives would be forever changed. This is what Jesus taught us to do. This is what Jesus commanded us to do.

So this journey into deliverance ministry has been what I call "brut-iful,"because it's brutal and beautiful—it produces times of sweetness, and it produces times of "shut up in Jesus' name!" But for me the most interesting transition has not been the transition of our entire church and tens of thousands of people online into this new level of ministry despite intense opposition, though that has been an epic experience. What amazes me most is the number of people and pastors and churches around the nation and the world that *aren't* being critical, but are reaching out in utter desperation, saying, "I thought I was crazy. I thought I was the only one seeing all this stuff in the Bible, and all of a sudden your church brought it to national attention. It's been hidden for so terribly long. Then finally you folks stood up and said, 'Let's just go for it. Let's just do what Jesus told us to do!'" I've heard that sentiment dozens of times, and it's good to know we're far from being alone in this awakening.

I think the reason it's working is because we really had to risk a lot to embrace it. We've made a lot of enemies out of people that used to be our friends. But that's OK, because that's always been true for the people who take Jesus at His word without compromise, come what may. Jesus said:

> Whoever is not with me is against me, and whoever does not
> gather with me scatters.
> —JESUS (MATTHEW 12:30, ESV)

There are two kingdoms, and they are at war with each other. There is a kingdom of Christ and a kingdom of the devil. Once and for all, we've got to figure out which side we are on. We can either go with what we know and risk it all to build the church God has called us to build, or we can go with what we're comfortable with and build the church this culture wants us to build.

We've finally come to grips with the reality that Jesus did this His entire ministry. The real gospel is divisive, and maybe we're not nearly as crazy as a lot of people think we are. They called Jesus a lot worse, and we're grateful to be in His company. If you are looking for true freedom in your life, or if you too are hearing the call to set people free, I hope you'll join us.

JESUS, THE SCARLET THREAD

As we turn toward the final chapter, I want to remind you of an overwhelming reality: it's all about Jesus. Psalm 40, which is a prophetic overture of Jesus, says, "Lo, I come: in the volume of the book it is written of me, I delight to do thy will, O my God" (vv. 7–8). The Bible is not about people, places, and things; it's about a single person. The whole Bible from cover to cover is all about one person, and that person is Jesus. There's a scarlet thread of the love of Jesus Christ in every story and every parable. In every syllable there is Jesus.

In Genesis, He's the seed of the woman. In Exodus, He's the rock. In Leviticus, He's the sacrificial lamb. In Numbers, He's the brazen serpent. In Deuteronomy, He's the Prophet. In Joshua, He's the captain of the Lord's hosts. In Judges, He's the great judge. In Ruth, He's our kinsman-redeemer. In 1 and 2 Samuel, He is the great king. In 1 and 2 Kings, He's the still, small voice of the ages. In 1 and 2 Chronicles, He's the bloodline of history. In Ezra, He's the pleading one. In Nehemiah, He's the building battler. In Esther, He's the unseen hand. In Job, He's the living Redeemer. In the Psalms, He's our Shepherd, our shield, and our strong tower. In Proverbs, He's wisdom personified. In Ecclesiastes, He's the fiery preacher. In Song of Solomon, He's the altogether lovely One.

In Isaiah, He's the Wonderful Counselor, mighty God. In Jeremiah, He's the weeping one. In Lamentations, He's our final authority. In Ezekiel, He is the watchman. In Daniel, He's the fourth man in the fire. In Hosea, He's the wedding groom. In Joel, He's the coming judge. In Amos, He's the plumb line. In Obadiah, He's the Mighty One. In Jonah, He's the ambassador. In Micah, He's the ruler of nations. In Nahum, He's the destroyer. In Habakkuk, He's the vision of God. In Zephaniah, He's the messenger of God. In Haggai, He's the Chosen One of God. In Zechariah, He's the Lord of hosts. In Malachi, He's the fulfillment of all prophecy.

In Matthew, He's the Son of Man. In Mark, He's the Son of God.

In Luke, He's our suffering Savior. In John, He's the magnificent Miracle Worker. In Acts, He's the builder of the church. In Romans, He's our justifier. In 1 and 2 Corinthians, He is our sufficiency. In Galatians, He's our burden bearer. In Ephesians, He's the fullness of the Godhead bodily. In Philippians, He's the servant. In Colossians, He's the preexistent One of all eternity. In 1 and 2 Thessalonians, He's the comer in the clouds. In 1 and 2 Timothy, He's the equipper of those in the ministry. In Titus, He's the One who cannot lie. In Philemon, He's the debt payer. In Hebrews, He's the great High Priest. In James, He's the object of our faith. In 1 and 2 Peter, He's the Bishop of our souls. In 1, 2, and 3 John, He's the Word of life. In Jude, He's the contender. In Revelation, He's King of kings and Lord of lords, the Alpha and Omega, the beginning and the end, the first and the last, the One that was, the One that is, and the One that ever shall be.

> Jesus said to him, "I am the way, and the truth, and the life. No one comes to the Father except through me."
> —JESUS (JOHN 14:6, ESV)

Chapter 15

DELIVERANCE MINISTRY

And I heard the voice of the Lord saying, "Whom shall I send,
and who will go for us?" Then I said, "Here I am! Send me."
—Isaiah 6:8, esv

A S YOU'LL RECALL from chapters 1 and 2, when the Holy
Spirit first called Tai and me into deliverance ministry, we
would have been lost without the work of the deliverance
generals who came before us. These saints endured the same persecution we do today but had very few allies to link up with, so I
will continually honor their work and encourage you to learn from
them as well. All you need to do is search the internet to find their
books and videos, and you can visit my website at LockeMedia.org
and navigate to *Support Resources* for suggestions and links. Praise
God that today we have a growing and diverse base of allies in this
battle, many of whom were featured in the film *Come Out in Jesus*
Name, so my website also has links to their resources.

Far more important, I want to help you get plugged into an
anointed deliverance ministry in your area so you can seek deliverance for yourself and your loved ones while also gaining continued training and support so you too can better do what Jesus
did. While it really is just a matter of commanding evil spirits to
come out in Jesus' name, as we've discussed in this text there is still
work to be done (before and after) to demolish strongholds and
ensure you keep the doors shut. For that, you can also navigate to

the Global Vision Freedom Network on my website to learn how our staff can help you in that regard while also getting you connected with the Global Vision hub closest to you and/or one of our partner churches in your area. Likewise, the body of Christ needs greater unity and with growing urgency, so that starts with each of us getting intentional about getting better connected. Our Freedom Network will do just that.

Of course, we encourage you to visit our main Global Vision Bible Church campus in Mount Juliet, Tennessee, just outside Nashville. We have worship services every Sunday morning and Wednesday night and a full-blown mass deliverance service every single Sunday night at 6 p.m. If you've seen *Come Out in Jesus Name*, you've seen these services in action. Hundreds drive in from all over the country (and some fly in from all over the world) every single week, so please know you are more than welcome to visit us anytime. Tai and I would love to meet you and your family. Since starting these services we've seen tens of thousands of people like you find freedom and gain better understanding to help their loved ones seek the ministry of Jesus as well.

FINDING FREEDOM NOW

While working with a minister with experience in deliverance ministry is always your best path, I want to equip readers as best I can right now. First, while we (and each of our allies in the major deliverance ministries) all have our own ways of approaching deliverance sessions, both on a one-on-one basis and in mass services, we must never forget that deliverance is not a methodology. There is no single "best" way to approach it, and since it all boils down to the work of the Holy Spirit through the authority of Jesus' name, it's far more important to be sensitive to His presence than to over-analyze the process. I've seen demons flee at the simple command in Jesus' name, and I've also seen demons beg and plead and even argue and scream for hours, so there are considerable variables that must be considered.

The spiritual state of the person going through deliverance is of paramount concern, as they should be fully repentant of their known sin and desperate for their freedom and release. Similarly, the ability to discern the spirits oppressing the person is invaluable. The Holy Spirit gives the gift of the discerning of spirits for very good reasons, so don't ever minimize the need for discernment through the process. Both of these variables underscore the great advantage of having a trained deliverance minister involved, so I will continue to encourage that path for all of you.

Beyond those, there are principles you can follow that will help set you on the right path for deliverance ministry, both as a recipient and a minister, and as we've learned in this book, Jesus calls us to engage in both. Whether you have been preaching for years or you're as green as Kermit the frog, these simple guidelines will help equip you to move in the right direction.

UNDERSTANDING THE FOUNDATION

Before engaging in deliverance ministry, you need to make sure you're standing on the solid ground of the truth. It is essential to be born again and establish a foundation rooted in biblical principles. Begin by studying the key scriptures discussed in this book. These passages are like signposts that point us in the right direction and lead us into deeper study while reminding us of the authority we've been given in the name of Jesus. We should continually remind ourselves that through Scripture we're handling the sword of the Spirit, so wield it often, and don't ever limit your study of the Bible to just these passages. We must dig deeper and gain a thorough understanding of the spiritual realm, including the reality of demonic forces and their strategies.

Underestimating the enemy's tactics and schemes can be deadly, so don't ever take any of this lightly. The more you learn about the spiritual realm, the better equipped you'll be to walk in victory and bring freedom to those who are bound. While this isn't a book on the named demons, demonology, or witchcraft, you can refer to *support resources* at LockeMedia.org for more information on those complex subjects.

Deliverance ministry is indeed simple, but it isn't a walk in the park. It takes personal preparation and spiritual maturity to step into those shoes. Before you try to minister to someone you believe is oppressed by dark spirits, you need to make sure you've taken the fundamentals above very seriously. Next, you need to stay engaged in daily prayer and regular fasting to seek God's guidance and to cultivate a deep relationship with Him. I'm not talking about cute little rote prayers. I'm talking about serious prayer (including praying in the Spirit, Romans 8:26) that connects you with the heart of God.

As an aid in this preparation, be sure you are very knowledge-able of the armor of God (Eph. 6:10–20) and remain well armored up at all times. Knowing that the armor is a scriptural metaphor that was given by God for spiritual warfare and daily righteousness, you should never take it off. The first book in this Spiritual Warfare Series, *Weapons of Our Warfare,* is a robust and rich guide that will help you fully understand how to use and activate each piece of armor to access its greatest power in daily living and in battle.

Finally, if you're preparing to minister to others, you must have gone through successful deliverance yourself. There's no point in trying to set others free if you are still in shackles of your own. For that, let's review the bottom-line basic elements that I deploy in every deliverance session. If someone seeking deliverance is born again and repentant of their sins, these are the bridges they need to cross to prepare to gain high ground in the battle.

Praying Into It

I always begin a deliverance session appealing to God in prayer, and so should you. I'll always ask the Holy Spirit to do the work that I cannot, and I also ask the Father to dispatch angels into the room because His Word says they are ministering spirits sent forth to minister to those who are the "heirs of salvation" (Heb. 1:14). I always recognize that we need His help from the spiritual realm, so I always ask Him to do what only He can do.

I then bind acts of witchcraft and curses that may be working against us, and I come against every word curse. Tai and I have both developed our ability to discern spirits to the point we can readily sense the spirits that are working against us during a session, so we always bind them during our initial prayer and continue binding and breaking them throughout a session as we continue to discern their activity. This, of course, is different for every session, which underscores the benefit of deeper training and spiritual development.

From there, I then command all the dark spirits—starting with the highest-ranking demons in the room—to reveal themselves in the name of Jesus, while ensuring they realize that I am not in any way afraid of them or intimidated by their presence. I boldly proclaim my authority in Jesus' name, and I forewarn them that they are coming up and coming out. Depending on what I'm discerning, and whether any spirit is already manifesting, I'll continue appealing to the Holy Spirit to remain engaged in the room, while continuing to declare my authority in Jesus' name over the dark spirits.

This prayer has no minimum or maximum time. I've prayed for a couple of minutes, and I've prayed for a half hour or more. I simply allow the Holy Spirit to lead me while discerning the spiritual condition of the room and the people. Through it all, I maintain my bold confidence in the authority of Jesus' name. Since there is no fixed methodology to follow, I will discuss the remaining basic elements in general terms, but please note that the "when" and how deeply I dive into each are determined in real time. In the early days I worked from a handbook that we published, but now I simply remain fluid and sensitive to the Holy Spirit's leading through every element.

PRAYER OF REPENTANCE, RENUNCIATION, AND AUTHORITY

After opening with prayer, I generally lead the person into praying repentance and making authoritative decrees in their own words. In mass deliverance services, I will help the people through this prayer by asking them to repeat after me, as every person needs to recognize the power of their speech and their personal responsibility to humbly repent with their own mouth. Remember, in the end we will overcome Satan through the blood of the Lamb and the word of our testimony, so our spoken words are crucial to that end. Here is an example of one of these prayers from a recent mass deliverance service that will show you the basic framework from which I build:

> *Holy Spirit, open my heart and my mind right now to any area of my life that is not fully surrendered to the lordship of Jesus Christ. If You show me now the areas of disobedience and rebellion in my life, I promise that I will repent and I will renounce them. I want to be free right now, in the mighty name of Jesus. I come against every evil spirit that is in resistance to my personal deliverance. I command them to be bound and rendered powerless. Any tormenting spirit trying to hinder my freedom in Christ must obey the authority of the name of Jesus and begin to leave me immediately.*
>
> *Satan, I resist you in Jesus' name, and I'm closing any and all doors which I or my ancestors may have opened*

to you and your demons. I renounce you, Satan, and I renounce all of your demons. I declare before God that you are my enemy. You are leaving my life now, completely and entirely, in Jesus' mighty name.

I am now claiming, by faith, deliverance from any and all evil spirits. I decree, by faith, that all curses which may be in me or around me are broken and revoked. And I now begin to demolish all strongholds, in Jesus' name. I take complete authority over it all right now, once and for all.

I close the door in my life to all occult practices, by me or against me, and I command, yes I command, every related spirit to come up and out of me now in the name of Jesus. I break all generational curses, spoken and unspoken, on both sides of my family going back twenty generations. I release myself immediately from every evil inheritance that I have ever received from my father or from my mother.

I renounce and break off every ungodly soul tie, and I repent for every immoral relationship in my life. Lord, I ask for Your forgiveness for any sexual immorality in my past or in my present. Other than my current spouse, I come out of agreement and I break covenant right now with every sexual partner I have ever had. I break those soul ties now. I settle those covenants now. I bind and abolish those relationships now. In the name of Jesus, I renounce all lust, perversion, immorality, all uncleanness, every form of impurity, adultery, fornication, pornography, and all other sexual sin.

I renounce my hatred and all of my anger, my resentment, my plans for revenge and retaliation, all forms of unforgiveness, and every ounce of bitterness. I renounce pride, the spirit of haughtiness, arrogance, vanity, and ego. I renounce disobedience and rebellion, all envy and jealousy, every form of fear, all doubt and worry, and every unbelief of Your Word.

I renounce any and all addiction to drugs and alcohol. I repent right now for any substance, legal or illegal, that I have ever allowed to keep me bound. I rebuke and call forth the spirit of pharmakeia. *In the mighty name of Jesus, I command you, spirit of* pharmakeia, *and every addiction that comes with you, to come all the way up and all the way out. I break every curse of addiction, and I bind every evil spirit of addiction. I will be free now, in the mighty name of Jesus.*

I renounce any affiliation with false religion and idolatry. I release myself and my entire family immediately from every curse that we have ever received or inherited through my bloodline from any and all false religions and belief systems. I renounce any connection, known or unknown, that my family or I have to any secret society, especially Freemasonry and the Masonic Lodge. I render these curses powerless now, in Jesus' mighty name.

I renounce every form of witchcraft, all sorcery, all spells, all divination, the python spirit, all occult involvement, all satanism, all New Age involvement, known or unknown, big or small, in the name of Jesus. I am coming against the spirit of witchcraft; you must come up and out of me now in the name of Jesus.

Based on information I learn in direct discussions or discern in the Spirit, I will always drill into the spirits discussed in this prayer as deeply as the Holy Spirit leads me, and this can go on for a very long time. The same is true of all other spirits I may discern through our time together. People who are oppressed by these spirits will generally manifest in some way, and the manifestations are wide and varied, but aside from an occasional effort to sprint away, these are typically of no real concern. The most common of these manifestations are crying, coughing, shaking, screaming, and light vomiting, but the list of possible reactions goes on and on. These manifestations can actually start up during the opening prayer, and some folks will even walk in the door manifesting. I simply remain fear-free, in the full authority of Jesus' name, and let the Holy Spirit lead from start to finish.

FORGIVENESS AND COMPASSION

As you'll recall from chapter 8, forgiveness is essential, as unforgiveness establishes a legal door for the tormentors. When people come to us for release and deliverance but still refuse to forgive someone, it's futile. For that, in every deliverance session I direct the people to finally forgive and release the people that hurt them, and I help them search their hearts and minds for any vestige of unforgiveness they may have tucked away.

And while we're at it, I direct them to release and forgive themselves of all the sins they have repented of and all the past mistakes that they have struggled to put behind them. I never rush this. Having been a pastor for thirty years, I have developed a high level of compassion and mercy for people, and I am sure to pour it out while they come to terms with their self-imposed bondage so they can finally forgive everyone and everything from their past, including themselves, and never look back. Once they do, deliverance is truly at hand.

Finally, I always ensure the person verbalizes their authority again before letting them leave, and in doing so I have them close all the doors, once and for all. In mass deliverance services, I will ask them to say a prayer like this:

> I command every evil spirit to depart from me right now.
> In the name of Jesus, I take authority over you. I will not
> be a victim, but a victor in Jesus Christ. So you'd better
> come up now. You'd better come out now. I take authority

over you this very moment. I completely banish you from
my life, and you can never return, in Jesus' name. Amen!

THE LOVE OF THE FATHER

If you've watched *Come Out in Jesus Name*, you'll remember the closing commentary from Tai concerning the love of the Father that she beautifully delivered during the final credit roll. Through the entire deliverance process, whether it lasts five minutes or five hours, the love of Father God must permeate every second, both through the recognition of His presence and through the heart and words of the deliverance minister. We can never forget, though we can find ourselves talking directly to demons within someone's flesh, the people they oppress are children of God who are deeply in need of compassion. We have to learn to separate the demon from its host and talk to each accordingly. I generally spend a lot of time ministering this overarching reality to them before, during, and after a deliverance session.

I always remind the person that perfect love casts out fear (1 John 4:18) and encourage them to get shrouded in the love of the Father and recognize that the Holy Spirit is desperately and deeply in love with them. The devil can't stand it when we know that we are covered in the love of Jesus, so that recognition is invaluable for both the deliverance and the healing that is to follow. I remind them that God loves them more than they will ever grasp, and that in His eyes they are not a failure, not a mistake, and not an accident. I tell them that God knew them before He formed them in the womb (Jer. 1:5) and call up Scripture to back all of this up the entire time we're together. If we come away from ministry without an increased knowledge of the love of the Father, the Son, and the Holy Spirit for us, in us, and through us, have we really found freedom? I think not.

GETTING PERSONAL

When ministering to folks in a one-on-one deliverance session, it's very helpful to gather important information about them, including their personal history, spiritual background, and areas they're struggling with. This helps us get a clear picture of what's going on and how to best help them. We try to cover all these bases in our conversations with them beforehand, as the more we know, the better we can discern the deeper things like the spirits that plague them.

Some deliverance ministers provide questionnaires for people to fill out, some simply ask questions as they prepare to minister to the person, and still others are so discerning of spirits that they can cut right to the chase in supernatural ways, but they'll still gain deeply personal information along the way. Because of the personal nature of the information gained, confidentiality must be maintained. We have to remember that people are trusting us with their deepest struggles, and it's our responsibility to maintain that trust. Ultimately, their freedom becomes part of their testimony, but they need to be the ones to determine when and if to go public with their praise report.

We can't ever forget that deliverance is just the beginning of the freedom and healing process. For that, we do all we can to continue walking alongside our brothers and sisters after they've been set free. That's why we started the Global Vision Freedom Network noted above. It's all about helping folks maintain their newfound freedom, continue to walk in victory, and grow their relationship with Jesus—and with others in the body of Christ. The other books in this Spiritual Warfare Series will prove to be amazing resources to help along the way.

Lastly, I strongly encourage you to engage in a remnant church that preaches deliverance, as that will prove priceless, while offering you a place to serve others in need of deliverance. For these signs shall follow them that believe: in Jesus' name they shall cast out devils! (Mark 16:17).

> And let us consider one another to provoke unto love and to good works: Not forsaking the assembling of ourselves together, as the manner of some is; but exhorting one another: and so much the more, as ye see the day approaching.
>
> —HEBREWS 10:24–25

CONCLUSION

I'VE GOT TO be honest: when you're in the midst of a full-blown revival for a considerable length of time, you begin to question the reality of when it's all going to stop. Ultimately, I know in my heart that it's a sovereign move of God, but I also wonder if He is ever going to lift His hand of blessing. But the phone calls for deliverance are still coming in every single day, and hundreds of visitors are still traveling to our church from all over the world, so it doesn't seem to be slowing down in any way. Everywhere I travel, crowds are gathering in ever-increasing numbers, and the people are desperately standing in line for deliverance, and it's always clear that it isn't about me. They're coming for the supernatural ministry of Jesus.

Normal church buildings aren't large enough to hold the people who show up, and most public venues are so uncomfortable with deliverance ministry that they won't let us book them, so it's getting increasingly difficult to manage it all. Pastors and ministry leaders from all over the world are reaching out to us to be set free, as are professional athletes and celebrities and people from every walk of life imaginable, and the amount of folks asking for training in the principles of deliverance ministry is truly astounding. We simply cannot keep up with the demand.

I never could have imagined that we would one day produce best-selling books and hit movies on the subject of deliverance from demons, but those are just evidence of what's really happening here. Personally, I am in the midst of the most surreal time of ministry that I've ever witnessed. The hunger for the supernatural power of God is beyond anything I could've ever imagined possible, so the critics can say what they want to. The haters can continue to hate. The religious zealots will forevermore try to discount and tear down what the Lord is doing, and that's OK. Jesus said it would be this way.

At the end of the day, God is going to get His glory and people are going to be set free on a massive scale. This deliverance revival is unstoppable because it's not about the leaders; it's about the wonder-working power of Jesus and the authority in His name. At this point, the movement has more momentum than virtually every other major move of God in the history of the church, and it's just the beginning. In the two thousand years since the days of Jesus, we've seen every type of revival imaginable, but not this. Deliverance is the revival element that has long been missing, and I believe it is the key to generating the sustaining power needed to ensure the revival never ends. When it's driven by the miracles of Jesus and power of the Holy Spirit, why would it?

Yes, it's messy. It's unconventional. It's unorthodox. It's non-religious. It's also the number one ministry of the Lord Jesus aside from preaching the gospel. We cannot discount what is happening, nor will we. To consider ever minimizing deliverance now or ever putting it back in the box is not only a ridiculous notion, but it would truly be an insurmountable task. The people would never allow it—nor would God. The lukewarm church in this age desperately needs a fresh infusion of the supernatural power of God, and just as it was in Jesus' ministry, this is where it begins.

The church has to stop preaching cute, motivational, pop psychology messages that simply make people feel good about themselves while leaving them bound in their sin, their rebellion, and their addictions. The restoration of the deliverance ministry of Jesus is the answer, and it's here to stay. Jesus said it was the very miracle that would signal that the kingdom of God has come to the earth, and here it is.

Deliverance ministry will not be silenced. Deliverance ministry will not be stopped. And deliverance ministry can no longer be overlooked. Deliverance ministry *is* revival. It should be shouted from the rooftops, and any church or any pastor that denies the power in the name of Jesus to cast out evil spirits needs to recognize that they're walking on the dangerous ground of biblical disobedience. Deliverance is not a game or a fad to be trifled with, but it will absolutely separate the serious followers of Christ from the cowards, for *these signs shall follow them that believe: in Jesus' name they shall cast out devils* (Mark 16:17). It's that simple. Demons are real. People are tormented, and the body of Christ is called, equipped, and commanded to see them set free. Rise up, saints; the kingdom of God is at hand! Demons know you have authority. They just hope you never awaken to that fact.

> So have no fear of them, for nothing is covered that will not be revealed, or hidden that will not be known. What I tell you in the dark, say in the light, and what you hear whispered, proclaim on the housetops.
>
> —JESUS (MATTHEW 10:26–27, ESV)

To be continued…

ABOUT THE AUTHOR

G REG LOCKE IS the founding and lead pastor of Global Vision Bible Church in Mount Juliet, Tennessee, just outside Nashville. He is the producer of the film *Come Out in Jesus Name* and host of the top-rated podcast *On Point With Pastor Greg Locke*. With a bachelor's degree in biblical studies and a master's degree in revival history, Locke is a revivalist and popular speaker in churches and political circles alike. He has achieved one of the largest social media platforms in the nation, and Global Vision has one of the broadest-reaching live stream ministries in the world. Locke and his wife, Taisha, work hand in hand in the ministry, seeking to reach those who are oppressed and forgotten by the church. They share six children and one grandchild.

Find us at LockeMedia.org.

Global Vision Press ™

READ MORE from the
SPIRITUAL WARFARE SERIES!

Thank you for reading *Cast It Out*. We hope this book has taught you about the power of the name of Jesus and the freedom and healing it can bring to every area of your life.

You can read more from Pastor Greg Locke's Spiritual Warfare Series with *Weapons of Our Warfare* and *Accessing Your Anointing*. Once you read this series in its entirety, you will be fully equipped to stand strong in the middle of all your spiritual battles.

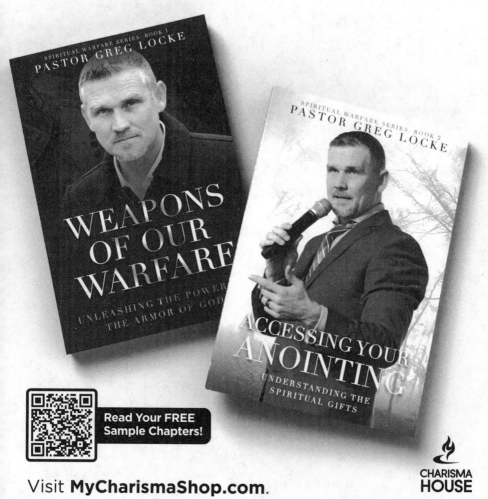